street food

street food

recreating the world's most authentic tastes

Tom Kime

Photography by Lisa Linder

London New York Munich
Melbourne Delhi

To my wife, Kylie Burgess Kime, for all her love and support, and for being such an
enthusiastic travel companion. To my mother, Helen, for being the inspiration behind my
love of food; to my father, Robert, for igniting my love of travel and discovery; and to my
sister, Hannah, for her ongoing curiosity and encouragement to pursue my goals.

Project Manager and Editor
Siobhán O'Connor

Senior Art Editor
Susan Downing

Photographic Art Direction and Design
Simon Daley

Senior Editor
Dawn Henderson

Photographer
Lisa Linder

Project Art Editor
Caroline de Souza

Home Economist and Food Stylist
Alice Hart

Editorial Assistant
Ariane Durkin

Prop Stylist
Victoria Allen

DTP Designer
Traci Salter

Design Assistance
Elly King and Sue Storey

Production Controller
Liz Cherry

First published in Great Britain in 2007 by Dorling Kindersley Limited
80 Strand, London WC2R 0RL

Penguin Group (UK)

Copyright © 2007 Dorling Kindersley
Text copyright © 2007 Tom Kime

2 4 6 8 10 9 7 5 3 1

A CIP catalogue record for this book is available from the British Library

ISBN: 978 1 4053 1580 7

Colour reproduction by Colourscan, Singapore
Printed and bound by Leo, China

Discover more at
www.dk.com

Contents

Toasted pitta bread salad • Courgette salad • Sesame
salad • Eastern jewelled pilaf with cinnamon and almonds •
Lamb meatballs with sour cherry sauce • Spinach pastries •
Spicy bean soup • Smoky roast aubergine dip • Yogurt
cream cheese dip • Carrot and orange salad with paprika
dressing • Lebanese lamb pizza • Coriander marinated fish
• Lamb kebabs with white bean and tomato salad •
Spinach and walnut salad • Spiced roast almonds • Libyan
pumpkin dip • Spiced tomato relish • Sesame tarator sauce
• Pine nut tarator sauce • Courgettes stuffed with lamb and
pine nuts • Houmous with cinnamon lamb • Spicy lamb
chops • Almond and cardamom biscuits

Recipe navigator

The recipe navigator is organized by type of dish, rather than by country of origin. You can see all the recipes at a glance and choose what you want to make, in combinations ranging from snacks and finger food, to dishes that are more substantial.

Best in a bowl

Mexican pumpkin flower soup pp100–1

Fresh, crisp salads

Toasted pitta bread salad pp156–7

Finger food

Masala popadums with tomato and green chilli pp24–5

Spicy seasoned potato in a cone pp28–9

Spicy fried okra pp32–3

Chaat with green chilli and pomegranate pp36–7

Summer rolls with prawns, crab, ginger, and mint pp44–5

Paper-wrapped chicken pp52–3

Singapore prawn fritters with sweet chilli sauce pp56–7

Crispy chicken spring rolls pp60–1

Hanoi prawn cakes pp74–5

Bean patties with avocado and tomato salad pp90–1

Semolina flour fritters pp114–15

Panelle (chickpea fritters) p115

Salt cod croquettes pp 130–1

Harissa mini fish cakes with preserved lemon pp 150–1

Spiced roast almonds pp180–1

salt cod croquettes
pp 30–1

A meal in itself

Spiced grilled chicken with coconut cream pp76–7

Poussin stuffed with olives, onion, and rosemary pp120–1

Pan-fried red mullet with preserved lemon, olives,
    and parsley pp124–5

Marinated quail with caper sauce pp132–3

Stuffed aubergine with yogurt and pine nuts p146

Stuffed fish balls p147

Eastern jewelled pilaf with cinnamon and almonds pp160–1

Lamb meatballs with sour cherry sauce pp162–3

Coriander marinated fish pp174–5

Lamb kebabs with white bean and tomato salad pp176–7

Courgettes stuffed with lamb and pine nuts pp186–7

Poussin stuffed with olives,
onion, and rosemary
pp 20–1

Hot wok and smoking grill

Chinese barbecue pork
pp66–7

Breads, pizzas, and savoury pastries

spinach pastries
pp164–5

Dips, sauces, and other condiments

Date and tamarind chutney p30

Fresh coriander and peanut chutney p31

Creamy coconut curry sauce p48

Fresh peach salsa pp94–5

Spicy vegetable pickle p96

Green tomato salsa pp104–5

Pipian sauce with cinnamon p106

Green cashew nut sauce p107

Roast pumpkin paste p154

Carrot pickle p155

Smoky roast aubergine dip p168

Yogurt cream cheese dip p169

Libyan pumpkin dip pp182–3

Spiced tomato relish p184

Tarator bi tahini (sesame tarator sauce) p185

Tarator bi sonoba (pine nut tarator sauce) p185

Houmous with cinnamon lamb pp188–9

Libyan pumpkin dip
pp182–3

Desserts and sweet treats

Banana and cinnamon pancakes pp80–1

Sweet potato and pumpkin doughnuts pp98–9

Pumpkin pudding pp108–9

Sweet fried ravioli pp122–3

Honey and nut pastries pp126–7

Date pastries pp138–9

Almond and cardamom biscuits pp192–3

Sweet potato and pumpkin
doughnuts pp98–9

The World Tour

The World Tour

To get a feel for the beating heart of any community, and to begin to understand a culture different from your own, you need to experience the food. In countries and regions famous for their cuisine, it is impossible to separate food from society. The food of the place is the identity, history, and social context cementing everyone together. It is a point of reference, and is used in poetry, literature, and music, as well as all aspects of human interaction. The cuisine links religion to the people, with feast days and holidays, and periods of fasting and remembrance. Regional variations bind the people to the land and the changing seasons, connecting them to their roots and heritage. The bounteous provision of food also reflects perceived wealth, but more importantly the generosity of the individual and the community. In a country such as Vietnam, where there is little material wealth, I have never met a more generous people – willing to share their food and pass on their culinary secrets. I experienced this generosity in people's homes from Ecuador to Lebanon, from Vietnam to Malta.

The best way to experience the real food that fuels and drives a community, however, is to sample the street food. The food from roadside stands, markets, open-air stalls, carts and wagons, and small cafés and bars captures the essence of life in that culture. This food is available 24/7, not just put on because there is a guest. It is real, robust, and a gauge of how people live and what values are important to the community. So how did I go about compiling a list of the best street food from at least five continents? Did I start with what I knew or what there was yet to discover? These were just two of the questions I asked myself in the initial stages of this book that was to take me to over 15 countries before my street food journey was completed.

I had already travelled extensively in Southeast Asia, so the food was familiar and the backbone of my cooking repertoire. My old loyalties to countries such as Italy also pulled at me. Yet instead I decided to start with countries in regions with which I was not familiar. Perhaps even more surprisingly, I started close to home. Actually, I started at home. My research – and hence my journey – began in London. This, it transpired, was the perfect place to gain inspiration from the ethnic groups who have carried their culinary heritage with them. More specifically, it was a great starting point for exploring the street food of India and Sri Lanka.

I have always been fascinated by Indian food with its use of spices and regional differences. I called my two friends Jaimin and Amandip Kotecha, who have a great nose for the restaurants specializing in regional Indian food that are dotted around London. We met in Kingsbury, and sat down to a spectacular feast of street food favourites from all over India. The food was amazing, and I scribbled copious

notes while eating my fill. My curiosity had been awakened. From this was born a long list of places that I had heard had great street food and, most importantly, that I had not yet visited.

The next step was Southeast Asia. When I first travelled to Thailand and Vietnam in my mid twenties, it completely knocked my socks off. I had never seen anything like it or tasted food like that before. Vietnamese food, in particular, is referred to as fragrant, aromatic, and perfumed. Vietnam has

"In countries and regions famous for their cuisine, it is impossible to separate food from society. The food of the place is the identity, history, and social context cementing everyone together. "

an amazing range of items from street food stalls, markets, and cafés, and so a number of recipes in this book come from this intoxicating country. Still in Southeast Asia, the cultural melting pot that is Singapore is famed for its hawker stalls. Chinese, Indian, and Malay food styles are all represented.

Where else would I go? I had always had an urge to visit South America because I love the rhythms of the music and dance that seem to be the backbone of all of Latin America. It is also the birthplace of many ingredients that we now see as mainstream across Western cuisine, such as potatoes, beans, corn, and chocolate. My journeys to South America and Mexico brought the recipes for the Latin America section, with a small side trip to Jamaica.

Southeast Asia was not the only region to exert its familiar pull on my taste buds and in turn the contents of the book. Reading *The Godfather* at an early age had started an obsession with Sicily that had not yet been fully realized. Sicilian cuisine yielded many of the recipes found in the Southern

Europe chapter. I thought I had a pretty good knowledge of Italian food, having travelled there often and also worked at the River Café in London for three years, where we changed the menu every lunch and dinner. Still, nothing could prepare me for the culinary treasures I was to find on this island, which were completely different from any other Italian food that I knew about. You can see the Moorish heritage in many dishes; Sicily's proximity to North Africa has had a profound influence on the unique food of this, the most-invaded island in the world.

North Africa and the Middle East have always intrigued me, too, because of the ancient spice routes and the traditional ways of living and cooking still largely intact from centuries past. Morocco conjures images of bazaars and spices, and probably has the most influential food of this region, so that was another "must do" destination. The food of the Levant region of the Eastern Mediterranean – namely Turkey, Lebanon, and Syria – has inspired centuries of food lovers and writers with its stunning flavours. It is an area that is special to my father. After years of hearing his stories and receiving gifts of spices, I wanted to see these places and taste their wonders for myself.

Of course, the rudimentary means by which much street food is served bears little resemblance to the actual make-up of the food itself. There is nothing unsophisticated about the complexity of the spices, seasonings, and flavours, or the variety of cooking techniques needed to present the finished dish. Be it a bowl, a plastic dish, or a plate fashioned from a banana leaf, it is packed full of delicious ingredients. I was frequently asked questions along the lines of: "What's the food like in South America?" This type

of question is impossible to answer because the different styles of food and eating that one can find in just one city or within one cultural group are enormous; once you travel further around a country, the variety simply expands. All around the world there are little snacks to be eaten while on the way to somewhere else. There are pastries, fritters, skewers, and wraps; salads, mezze, and tapas. Soups are served at all times of the day. Stews, casseroles, and tagines are slow-cooked to blend complex flavours. Fresh fish, kebabs, or strips of meat are quickly cooked over glowing embers. Large cuts and whole animals are baked in wood ovens, grilled, or spit-roasted. Regional variations of breads, relishes, and dips alone abound. Most things that I sampled were well made and freshly cooked, and I could witness them being enjoyed by

"I often started at the main vegetable market, then the fish market or where the fishing boats came into port. Another good location was near the central bus station or railway station."

the locals. In all the places that I visited, the reality was that there was no such thing as bad food sold from little stalls. If it were bad, no one would buy it, and the vendor would soon be out of business. Sometimes I would see two stalls close together. One would have a lively buzz and be packed with people buying the delights on offer; the other would be practically empty. My choice was obvious.

When I arrived in unfamiliar towns and cities, I often started at the main vegetable market, then the fish market or where the fishing boats came into port. Another good location was near the central bus station or railway station. I would head in the opposite direction to the throng of tourists, instead

following the locals to see how and where they bought their meals. One of the best indicators of the local hotspots is the workers, who are very discerning. Wherever the postmen, policemen, bus drivers, cyclo drivers, market traders, or fishermen are communing to eat, chances are it will be one of the best places in the neighbourhood and worth a look. I had many great conversations with taxi drivers in different countries, and became practised in asking what their favourite food was. I would ask where the food was sold and whether they could take me there, whatever the time of day or night.

A common thread that seems to run throughout all the countries and places renowned for their street food is that the people seem to be completely obsessed with eating it, planning to eat it, or talking about it. I often ate at 2am or started in the market at 5.30 or 6am. In Beirut, my friend Talal was completely unfazed at the idea of eating five breakfasts between 7am and 10.30am. There is much on offer and it is all deliciously tasty and handmade. Street food is fresh and usually healthy. If it is not healthy, it is so scrumptious that you do not really care.

The recipes that follow were chosen through much travelling and tasting. The list of countries they sprang from came out of places that interested me, in the context of social history and what I refer to as the "anthropology of food". The cuisines chosen have evolved over centuries of conquest, invasion, and migration. The countries visited share another thing: a healthy obsession with food and eating. It may seem like an eclectic list, and it is by no means a comprehensive one, but it is my personal street food journey through countries that have fascinated travellers for centuries. I hope it inspires you.

India and Sri Lanka

The cuisine of the Indian subcontinent and Sri Lanka has vast regional variety. From the Himalayas to the palm-fringed beaches in the tropical south, local food changes with the climate, terrain, religion, and many different languages. The bounty of street food reflects these contrasts. Opposite flavours are often put together to draw out their distinctive characteristics such as hot and sweet, or salty and sour. Texture is important, too. Also, a hot dish may be served with a cool dressing, or vice versa. Traditionally people order a selection of dishes reflecting a range of intensity of spices from mild to very hot.

Day 1: London, United Kingdom I was determined to explore further the depth and variety of street food that emanates from India and Sri Lanka, when it occurred to me that the perfect place to start was in my own back yard. London, with its large and vibrant Indian and Sri Lankan communities, was sure to provide ample opportunity for authentic fare. When you live in a large city such as London, you are often familiar with only a relatively small area. Boroughs and suburbs that are not your usual stomping ground may seem very foreign. Kingsbury in the northwest of London was such an area for me; however, for my good friends Jaimin and Amandip Kotecha it housed one of their favourite restaurants. The brightly lit eatery serves authentic Indian street food specialities. My hosts rattled off their favourites to the waiter, then added the dishes that they wanted me to try because they were house specials or particularly authentic to certain regions. The waiter turned the page on his notebook and suggested we move to a larger table that could cope with the gluttony that was about to commence. The restaurant filled with respected local businessmen and large families with members from every generation, and I was the only blond in sight. At this point I relaxed, as I knew I was going to get the good stuff, not the food altered for pedestrian Western tastes.

Day 7: Malta As executive chef of a restaurant called Taste at the Fortina Spa Resort on the island of Malta, I have made many visits to set up the restaurant, train my staff, and change and update the menus. During this time, I have become friends with Ratnesh, who manages the excellent Indian restaurant at the Fortina. When I said that I was researching street food for my book, he generously invited me to his house for a tasting. He and his wife produced stunning morsels that were common street food in their native Mumbai. Every component of the meal, which went on for hours, was delicious. The two recipes for *chaat* (slang for "street food") given on pp28–9 and pp36–7 were made with me hovering by the pan with notebook and pen in hand. The chutney had been made that afternoon, and I had to stop myself from eating it out of the jar. There was a constant stream of fresh flavours straight from the hot pan; a mix of vibrant colours and textures such as pomegranate seeds and fried sprouted beans were eaten in the blink of an eye. The whole experience taught me about the freshness and simplicity of much of Indian food and fitted perfectly with my theory that the best food stimulates all our senses.

Masala papad Masala popadums with tomato and green chilli

Serves 6

2 teaspoons ground cumin

3 tomatoes

1 onion, finely chopped

2 fresh green chillies, deseeded and
  finely chopped

1 teaspoon medium red chilli powder

juice of 2 limes

½ bunch of fresh coriander, leaves picked

12 popadums or about 24 mini popadums
  (use freshly cooked or store-bought)

salt and freshly ground black pepper

One characteristic of Indian street food is the plentiful combination of textures, temperatures, and contrasting flavours. This simple example has all of those elements present to delicious effect, and you can make this dish while preparing the rest of the ingredients for a larger meal. It is then simply scattered over the popadums before serving. The secret to this dish is that it must be eaten straight away, otherwise the popadums will become soggy. Alternatively, use another Indian-style bread such as naan, to make the snack a bit more substantial.

1 Put the ground cumin in a small dry frying pan, and toast over a medium heat for about 2 minutes until aromatic.

2 Halve the tomatoes, remove the seeds, and cut the flesh into fine dice. Mix the tomato and onion in a bowl with the green chilli. Season well with salt and pepper. Add the toasted cumin powder and the chilli powder, then stir in the lime juice. Scatter over the coriander leaves and gently stir through.

3 When ready, scoop some of the mixture onto each of the popadums, and serve immediately.

Moily haldi
Coconut and turmeric fish soup

This fantastically tasty fish soup hails from Sri Lanka and the southern coastal regions of India. When I first tasted it, I found it very difficult to identify the source of its striking richness. It was only when I asked how it was made that I discovered that the soup was thickened with a paste made from cashew nuts. The nuts are lightly roasted, then ground into a paste with chopped coriander stems. I have since learned that this technique is frequently used to enrich soups, stews, and curries for special occasions.

Serves 4–6

2 tablespoons vegetable oil

45g (1½oz) raw cashew nuts

2 garlic cloves, finely chopped

5cm (2in) piece of fresh root ginger, peeled and finely chopped

2 small fresh red chillies, deseeded and finely chopped, plus extra, cut into slivers, to serve (optional)

1 bunch of fresh coriander, leaves picked and stems finely chopped

2 onions, finely chopped

1 tablespoon fennel seeds

1 tablespoon coriander seeds

1 teaspoon ground turmeric

1 litre (1¾ pints) good-quality fish stock

300ml (10fl oz) coconut cream

2 teaspoons muscovado sugar

juice of 2 limes

400g (14oz) baby squid, cleaned

400g (14oz) large uncooked prawns, peeled, deveined, and halved lengthways

500g (1lb 2oz) firm white-fleshed fish, cut into bite-sized chunks

salt and freshly ground black pepper

1 Heat a heavy frying pan over a medium heat. Add 1 tablespoon of the oil, and lightly brown the cashew nuts. Set aside. In the same oil, fry the garlic, ginger, and chopped chilli for 2–3 minutes until fragrant. Pound the cashew nuts, chopped coriander stems, and fried spices using a pestle and mortar, to make a paste. Set aside. Heat the remaining oil in a clean heavy pan over a low heat. Add the onion. Gently fry for 10 minutes until the onion is soft.

2 Meanwhile, crush the fennel and coriander seeds using a pestle and mortar. When the onion is soft, add the fennel and coriander seeds and the turmeric. Fry for 2 minutes until fragrant. Add half the cashew paste. Pour in the fish stock and coconut cream, then add the sugar and season with salt and pepper. Simmer for 10 minutes. Add the lime juice and remaining nut paste. Taste and adjust the seasoning. It should have a balance of sweet richness and acidity.

3 While the soup base is simmering, slit the squid open and, using a small sharp knife, carefully score the outside in a crisscross pastern. Cut the squid into smaller pieces. Put in a bowl with the prawns and fish. Season well with salt and pepper. Add to the soup, and simmer for 3 minutes until the prawns turn pink and the squid is opaque. Stir in half of the coriander leaves. Serve at once in small bowls garnished with the coriander leaves and extra red chilli (if using).

Chaat Ratnesh
Spicy seasoned potato in a cone

Serves 8

3 waxy potatoes

2 tablespoons flaked coconut

a little vegetable oil

1 onion, finely chopped

200g (7oz) mixed mung bean sprouts and
   alfalfa sprouts, rinsed and drained

2 fresh green chillies, deseeded and
   finely chopped

1 red pepper, seeds and membrane
   removed, finely diced

juice of 1 lemon

2 spring onions, finely sliced

3 tablespoons date and tamarind chutney
   (see p30)

30 fresh coriander leaves, roughly chopped

salt and freshly ground black pepper

1 First make the cones to hold the filling; these will take the greatest amount of time, so it is better to have them all ready before you start cooking. You will need some banana leaves. Cut them into 10cm x 20cm (4in x 8in) rectangles, allowing enough for 3 per person. Roll each rectangle into a tight cone. Secure the edges with a toothpick to hold in place.

2 Peel the potato and cut into 1cm (½in) chunks. Put into a pan of cold water with a little salt and bring to the boil. Reduce the heat and simmer until soft to the point of a knife, but still firm. Drain in a sieve and leave to cool.

3 Place a dry heavy pan over a medium-high heat. Add the coconut and toast until golden brown. Remove and set aside. Add a little oil to the pan, and fry the onion for 3–4 minutes until golden brown. Increase the heat to high, add the bean sprouts, and fry quickly for a further 2 minutes. Next add the chilli and red pepper. Cook quickly for another couple of minutes so that the mixture still has a good bite to it. Season well with salt and pepper. Add the lemon juice and stir through gently.

4 Combine the cooked mixture with the diced potato, spring onion, and date and tamarind chutney. Add the coriander and stir through. Taste and adjust the seasoning. The seeds and coconut should provide a good crunch. Using a small spoon, fill the cones and hand them to your guests with small teaspoons to eat the filling. Eat immediately so that the filling does not soften the cone. You can refill the banana-leaf cones if required.

My friend Ratnesh introduced me to this quick and tasty Indian street food snack, or "chaat". It is incredibly good and, like much Indian food when it is made well, healthy and easy. This particular chaat mixture is stuffed into small cones fashioned from banana leaf. Banana leaves are available in Asian food stores. You could also ask your greengrocer to order them for you with a bit of notice. If you can't find fresh banana leaves, make small cones using baking parchment or even coloured craft paper or something similar.

Khajar imli chatni
Date and tamarind chutney

This is a strong aromatic relish which is deliciously rich and complex. There is lots of spice; you could add more chilli if you liked. The use of tamarind and vinegar means that this pickle will be predominately hot, sour, and sweet. This chutney is great alongside roasted meats or a curry, and it is often served as an accompaniment to street food dishes, with their contrasting textures and balance of flavours. It goes especially well with Chaat Ratnesh (see pp28–9).

Makes about 4 jars

100g (3½oz) fresh root ginger, grated
6 fresh red chillies, deseeded and
  finely chopped
4 garlic cloves, finely chopped
1kg (2¼lb) pitted dates, roughly chopped
1 tablespoon coriander seeds
1 tablespoon cumin seeds
4 green cardamom pods
2 teaspoons ground cinnamon

1 teaspoon ground nutmeg
1 teaspoon ground cloves
250g (9oz) onions, finely chopped
200g (7oz) tomatoes, chopped
200g (7oz) soft brown sugar
250g (9oz) sour tamarind pulp
  (see note below)
250ml (9fl oz) malt vinegar
sea salt and freshly ground black pepper

1 Pulse the ginger, chilli, and garlic in a food processor until you have a thick pulp. Add half the dates and process until they are roughly puréed. (Leave the other half roughly chopped.) Toast the coriander seeds, cumin seeds, cardamom pods, cinnamon, nutmeg, and cloves in a small heavy pan over a medium-high heat for 2–3 minutes until aromatic. Remove from the pan, and grind until smooth using a pestle and mortar, or a spice grinder. Pass through a sieve to get rid of any coarse woody husks.

2 Put all the ingredients, including the spice powder and date mixture, in a heavy pan. Add 500ml (16fl oz) water, and cook down slowly for 1–2 hours to make a thick dark relish. Stir frequently to avoid the sugar catching on the bottom of the pan. Taste and season well with salt and pepper. This chutney can be eaten straight away or bottled in sterilized glass jars with secure-fitting lids. Store in a cool, dark place, and keep refrigerated once opened.

Using tamarind Tamarind is available in various forms. It can be bought in a block, which contains the flesh, stone, and stringy fibres. To use this, place in a bowl and pour over 500ml (1¾ pints) boiling water. Allow the mixture to cool, then break up the sticky pieces, pressing the stones away from the flesh with your fingers. Discard any stones and tough fibres. Add another 500ml water and pass it all through a sieve. This is tamarind pulp. Alternatively, you can buy jars of pulp already prepared. There is also a tamarind concentrate available; this needs to be diluted with water because it is very black and very strong.

Patta moongphali chatni

Fresh coriander and peanut chutney

Serves 6–8

3 tablespoons skinless raw peanuts

1 garlic clove, peeled

½ teaspoon salt

1 teaspoon sugar

1 teaspoon ground cumin

1 teaspoon ground coriander

4 medium-hot fresh green chillies, deseeded
and finely chopped

1 large bunch of fresh coriander, roughly
chopped

juice of 2 limes

1 Roast the peanuts in a dry frying pan until golden brown, taking care they do not scorch. Remove from the heat, and allow to cool before placing in a food processor with the garlic, salt, sugar, cumin, and ground coriander. Process to a paste. Add the green chilli, fresh coriander, and 2 tablespoons water. Process until a smooth purée or leave with a bit of texture, according to your taste.

2 Place the fresh herb mixture in a bowl, and add the lime juice. Taste and adjust seasoning. It should be hot from the chilli, sweet from the roasted nuts, and salty and sour from the lime juice. Use straight away.

Fresh herb chutneys such as this one are commonly used in Sri Lanka and India to accompany grilled fish, meat, or shellfish. There are many variations using peanuts, cashew nuts, or fresh or roasted coconut. The sourness is usually supplied by using lemon juice, lime juice, or fresh tamarind pulp. It should be eaten immediately, as the acidity of the citrus juice will start to cook the fresh green herbs. It can be used to marinate grilled prawns or fresh tuna, or served on the side like a relish. It would be great as part of a summer barbecue or with prawn or chicken skewers.

Bhindi chatpatti Spicy fried okra

Serves 4–6

2 tablespoons Greek-style yogurt

200g (7oz) gram flour (chickpea flour)

1½ teaspoons chilli powder

1 teaspoon ground cumin

1kg (2¼lb) fresh okra

300ml (10fl oz) vegetable oil

sea salt and freshly ground black pepper

lemon wedges, to finish

Okra, or bindhi, is cooked in many different ways in all sorts of Sri Lankan and Indian dishes. For best results it should be fried in a little oil until golden brown with a nutty taste, then added to other vegetables or covered with a sauce. This recipe is very simple and is eaten as a snack in many parts of Sri Lanka and India. When I first had okra this way, I found them so delicious that it was difficult for me to stop eating them. They are very moreish and work well at the start of a larger meal.

1 To make the batter, spoon the yogurt into a large bowl. Sift in the gram flour and mix together using a whisk. Add the chilli powder and ground cumin. Continue whisking while slowly adding the cold water. The batter should be the consistency of double cream. If it is too thin, simply add a little extra yogurt. Season well with salt and pepper, then leave the batter to stand while you prepare the other ingredients.

2 Cut the okra in half lengthways. Place in a colander and rinse thoroughly under cold water. Leave for a few minutes, then give the colander a good shake to drain off any excess water. Turn out the okra onto a clean, dry tea towel, and pat dry to get rid of all the moisture.

3 Heat the vegetable oil in a heavy pan over a medium heat. To test that the oil is hot enough, coat a piece of okra in the batter and drop into the oil. It should sizzle immediately; if it doesn't, allow the oil to get hotter before adding any more okra. When the oil is ready, take a handful of okra and dip into the batter. Carefully drop the battered okra into the hot oil, scattering them across the surface of the oil so that they do not stick together. (It is important to cook the okra in batches; otherwise the temperature of the oil will drop and the okra will become soggy.) Move the okra around the pan, separating them with a slotted spoon, and fry for about 3 minutes until golden brown all over. Remove from the oil and drain well on kitchen paper so that they are not too greasy. Keep warm while you continue cooking in batches until all the okra is used.

4 Sprinkle with sea salt and serve in a large stack with lemon wedges to squeeze over – the acidity of the lemon complements the spicy okra. Alternatively, make small paper cones, securing the edges with toothpicks. Fill each one with some of the fried okra, and finish with a squeeze of lemon juice before serving straight away.

Tawa mooli paratha Crispy paratha

Makes 8

For the dough

125g (4½oz) sifted wholewheat flour

125g (4½oz) sifted plain flour

2 teaspoons salt

For the filling

1 daikon (mooli or Japanese radish), about
   15cm (8in) long, grated

1 tablespoon cumin seeds

1 tablespoon coriander seeds

4 spring onions, finely sliced

4 cm (1¾in) piece of fresh root
   ginger, grated

2 fresh green chillies, deseeded
   and finely chopped

½ bunch of fresh coriander,
   roughly chopped

salt and freshly ground black pepper

100g (3½oz) butter, melted, for cooking

Paratha is a staple Indian flat bread with a flaky texture. It originates from the northwestern Indian province of Punjab. Here there are many types of bread that are eaten at all times of the day. Paratha can be eaten plain or can be stuffed with all manner of fillings, from meat to vegetables or pulses. They are often eaten for breakfast with spicy pickles and fresh yogurt. The stuffing can be simple like this street-food version or much more elaborate for feast days and banquets, such as spiced lamb and pomegranate seeds.

1 To make the dough, sift the two flours into a large bowl and add the salt. Make a well in the centre, slowly pour in 250ml (8fl oz) water, and mix into a dough. Turn onto a lightly floured work surface. Knead well for 10 minutes. Return the dough to the bowl, and cover with a damp cloth. Rest for 45 minutes.

2 Meanwhile, prepare the filling. Place the daikon on a clean tea towel, and squeeze all the liquid out until it is bone dry. Toast the cumin and coriander seeds in a small dry frying pan over a medium heat for 2 minutes until aromatic. Crush the seeds using a pestle and mortar, or a spice grinder. Mix all the filling ingredients together, and season well with salt and pepper.

3 Once the dough has rested, divide into 8 equal-sized balls. Knead each one again for a couple of minutes. Roll each dough ball into a disc about 8cm (3½in) in diameter. Place a spoonful of filling in the centre of each disc. Fold the edges into the centre to cover the filling completely, then give the gathered edges a slight twist to seal the bundle shut. Turn over so that the sealed side is facing down. Gently roll until the paratha is about twice its original width.

4 Heat a heavy pan over a medium-high heat. Slap a paratha into the pan and cook for 30 seconds. Turn over and cook for a further 30 seconds. Brush with melted butter and turn again. Press down with a spatula, brush with more melted butter, then flip again, cooking for 30 seconds each time. Flip a couple of times more, leaving for about 10 seconds each time. Cook for 3 minutes in all, until golden brown with a couple of dark spots. Cut into wedges and serve.

Chaat anardana hari mirch

Chaat with green chilli and pomegranate

In Mumbai, a slang word for street food snacks is "chaat". Snacks such as this are eaten all over India at any time of the day, and there are hundreds of varieties. They often have a very noticeable contrast in tastes between hot, sweet, salty, and sour. This particular chaat is served on toasted naan or pitta bread. Alternatively, you could use fried pieces of samosa dough, which can be bought at any Indian grocery store. You could even serve it on popadums broken into small triangles. It makes a striking canapé to impress your guests.

Serves 6

a little vegetable oil

2 garlic cloves, finely chopped

½ teaspoon dried chilli flakes

1 small onion, finely chopped

200g (7oz) mixed sprouted mung beans
and alfalfa sprouts, rinsed and drained

1 orange

1 apple

1 pomegranate

3 spring onions, finely sliced

2 fresh green chillies, deseeded and
finely chopped

½ bunch of fresh coriander, roughly
chopped

naan or pitta bread, cut into triangular
pieces and toasted, to serve

Fresh mango chutney

1 ripe mango, peeled and finely diced

2 fresh red chillies, deseeded and
finely diced

½ teaspoon ground cumin

1 tablespoon soft brown sugar

2 tablespoons tamarind pulp

salt and freshly ground black pepper

1 Heat a little oil in a heavy frying pan over a medium-high heat. Fry the garlic and dried chilli until aromatic. Add the onion and cook quickly until soft and just starting to colour. Add the sprouts. Keep frying quickly, stirring, for 2–3 minutes. Remove from the heat and tip into a bowl. Peel the orange and segment it, removing any pith. Cut the orange flesh into small dice, then finely dice the apple. Add the orange and apple to the sprout mixture.

2 To remove the seeds from the pomegranate, take the fruit in your left hand and tap firmly all over with a wooden spoon. Cut the pomegranate in half, hold each half over the bowl of sprout mixture, and continue to firmly tap the outside of the fruit. The seeds will fall out, leaving the bitter white pith behind. Next add the spring onion, chilli, and coriander. Stir through.

3 Put all the chutney ingredients in a small saucepan. Add 100ml (3½fl oz) water and bring to the boil. Reduce the heat, and simmer for 12–15 minutes or until the excess water has evaporated. Remove from the heat, and cool. Spoon about 3 tablespoons of the chutney onto the sprout mixture as a dressing. The mixture is then spooned onto the naan bread and eaten immediately. If you are serving as canapés, don't add the topping until the last minute.

Aloo jeera
Potato and cumin curry

This classic potato curry from South India is a dish that frequently features as street food. It works very well as an accompaniment to other curries and dishes, so that you have a selection of different flavours, colours, and textures. Fresh home-made curries taste so different from takeaway and those served in restaurants, and you can truly appreciate the essential simple nature of true Indian food.

Serves 4–6

2 tablespoons vegetable oil

4 garlic cloves, crushed

4cm (1¾in) piece of fresh root
  ginger, grated

100g (3½oz) shallots, finely chopped

450g (1lb) potatoes, peeled and
  cut into 1cm (½in) dice

1 teaspoon ground turmeric

1 tablespoon black mustard seeds

1 tablespoon ground coriander

1 tablespoon ground cumin

2 green cardamom pods

3 fresh green chillies, deseeded
  and finely chopped

4 tomatoes, chopped into chunks

300g (10oz) can chickpeas, drained
  and rinsed in cold water

1 teaspoon salt

juice of 1 lemon

½ bunch of fresh coriander

freshly ground black pepper

1 Heat the oil in a heavy saucepan over a medium-high heat. Add the garlic and ginger. Fry for 2–3 minutes until the garlic and ginger are fragrant. Add the shallot and potato, and stir-fry for about 4 minutes until the shallot has softened. Stir in the turmeric, mustard seeds, ground coriander, cumin, and cardamom. Cook for 1 minute until the spices are fragrant, then add the chillies, tomato, and chickpeas. Add 4 tablespoons water and the salt, season with pepper, and cover the pot. Continue cooking over a medium-high heat for about 20 minutes until the potato is soft to the point of a knife.

2 To finish, add the lemon juice and half the coriander. Taste the curry – it should have a good balance of spicy, sweet, sour, and salty. Adjust the seasoning if necessary. Garnish with lots of fresh coriander and serve as part of a larger selection of curries, grilled fish or meat, dips, and Indian breads.

Southeast Asia

Southeast Asia gives to the world a myriad
of cuisines and culinary influences, with
traditions often spanning generations. Yet
governing all these there still remain distinct
boundaries that give each country or cultural
group its trademark food. For instance, there
are four main tastes found in Vietnamese
cuisine: hot, sweet, salty, and sour. This basic
structure is apparent in every dish and every
mouthful. In Thailand, this is called "rot chart",
or "correct taste". In Singapore, the food
reflects the extraordinary melting pot that
is this small island nation. Binding all these
regions is a culture of street food coupled with
an explosion of tastes, flavours, and aromas
guaranteed to tempt the palate.

Day 11: Singapore Arriving in steamy Singapore five days before Christmas, after a long and squashed flight from wintry London, was more than a little disorienting. Suddenly it was sticky and humid, and the middle of the night – but I had a limited number of days in which to ingest the food of Singapore and wanted to begin my mission immediately. One of the best ways to find the most delicious local street food is to ask the taxi drivers. I had heard about roti prata (pp46–7) from a friend who had worked as a journalist in Singapore. Now, despite the late hour, I was determined to find it. I dropped my bags off at the hotel, and asked my taxi driver to take me to the best stall of roti prata in Singapore. He set off, but the streets seemed ominously quiet and ghostlike, empty of the hungry locals I hoped to join. Five dollars later we turned a corner and all was explained. A small café was acting like a beacon in the night, its canary yellow plastic tables and stark fluorescent lights welcoming all prospective diners – and there were hundreds. For the length of the block there was no footpath to be seen – only happy faces seated at flimsy chairs and tables devouring their favourite dish. And this was at 1.30am on a Tuesday. Welcome to Singapore. I sat down, and finally my roti prata arrived. I tore it into pieces, dipped it into a spicy curry sauce, and devoured. With one mouthful I knew exactly where I was. Heaven.

Day 14: Hue, Vietnam Vietnam is an extraordinary country, with a unique cuisine. Leaving the organized chaos of Hanoi in the north, I head for the ancient imperial city of Hue, situated on the banks of the Perfume River. Hue is well kept and has a rare tranquillity. It is a strange type of silence. The city suffered 10,000 fatalities under American bombardment as a response to the North Vietnamese Tet Offensive in the spring of 1968, and has never quite recovered. Much of the ancient citadel was destroyed, yet you can still imagine its former splendour. Despite Hue's renown for elaborate and intricate displays of tradition, the most delicious meal that I ate there was the simplest: *bahn khoai*, or happy crêpes. These mouth-watering open pancakes are stuffed with pork and prawns and mushrooms. I found this dish in the establishment of a man who is a deaf mute, and expresses his love through his food. Mr Le of Lac Tien is extraordinarily welcoming; we ate and laughed all afternoon. His mother, who opened the restaurant 35 years ago, made the pancakes, and his children all served, and laughed at my long legs while practising their English.

Goi cuon Summer rolls with prawns, crab, ginger, and mint

Summer rolls are eaten all over Vietnam at small cafés, roadside restaurants, and stalls. Quite different from fried spring rolls, they are a refreshing burst of flavours and textures. Excellent as a snack or canapé, or at the start of a larger meal, they come in many different seasonal and regional variations. Texture is very important in Vietnamese cooking and, with the firm, springy prawns, tender crabmeat, and crisp fresh vegetables and herbs, you have everything going on in one contained mouthful. They are so juicy you don't really need a dipping sauce.

Serves 4–6

100g (3½oz) dried rice vermicelli (thin rice noodles)

½ cucumber

12 cooked fresh prawns (not frozen), peeled and deveined

3 tablespoons cooked white crabmeat (use fresh-picked crabmeat if possible)

10 fresh mint leaves, chopped

2 spring onions, cut into slivers

2cm (¾in) piece of fresh root ginger, grated

juice of 1 lime

2 tablespoons light soy sauce

2 tablespoons fish sauce

12 or so rice paper wrappers (available from Asian grocers or gourmet food shops)

salt and freshly ground black pepper

1 Put the vermicelli in a large bowl and cover with boiling water. Leave to soak for about 5 minutes while you prepare the rest of the filling.

2 Thinly slice the cucumber, leaving the seeds in the centre untouched. Stack the cucumber slices, then cut into thin matchsticks. If wrapping your summer rolls in a cone shape, leave the prawns whole; if using the more usual spring-roll shape, halve or finely slice if large. Mix everything except the vermicelli and rice paper wrappers in a bowl. Drain the vermicelli, cut into smaller lengths using kitchen scissors, and add to the bowl. Season with salt and pepper, and stir through. Adjust seasoning.

3 Soak the rice paper wrappers, about 5 at a time, in warm water for 20 seconds or until softened. (Be careful that they don't stick together, as they tear easily.) Lay out 4 or 5 wrappers side by side on a clean damp tea towel on a flat surface – this keeps the wrappers pliable. Place a tablespoon or so of the filling on each wrapper about 2.5cm (1in) from the bottom edge and in the centre, leaving 2.5–5cm (1–2in) of wrapper on either side. To make a cone, fold one side of the wrapper towards the centre; to make a spring roll, fold both sides towards the centre. Fold the bottom edge facing you over the top of the mixture and, using firm pressure, roll up so the filling is enclosed. (Top up the cones with a little extra filling if needed.) Place on a tray covered with another clean damp cloth. Repeat the process until the filling has run out. Cover tightly with cling film until needed, to prevent the wrappers drying out.

Roti prata Chicken-stuffed flat bread

Makes 12–14

500g (1lb 2oz) plain flour, sifted

1 teaspoon sea salt

1 teaspoon caster sugar

4 tablespoons lukewarm milk

about 150g (5½oz) melted butter

2 fresh green chillies, deseeded and
   finely chopped

2 garlic cloves, finely chopped

1 teaspoon ground cinnamon

1 teaspoon ground coriander

200g (7oz) shredded cooked chicken

2 onions, finely chopped

3 tomatoes, finely chopped

a little beaten egg for brushing

a little vegetable oil

salt and freshly ground black pepper

1 Combine the flour, salt, and sugar in a mixing bowl. Add 125ml (4½fl oz) lukewarm water, the milk, and 2 tablespoons of the melted butter, and combine. Knead gently with your hands for about 7 minutes, adding more water or flour as needed to create a soft dough. Pinch off pieces the size of large limes and shape into balls. Roll in the remaining melted butter to coat, then place on a plate. Cover with cling film, and let stand in a cool place for about 45 minutes.

2 For the stuffing, heat a little oil in a frying pan over a medium-high heat. Fry the chilli, garlic, cinnamon, and coriander for 2 minutes until fragrant. Stir in the chicken, onion, tomato, and salt and pepper to taste. Set aside.

3 Lightly grease a large chopping board with some extra melted butter. Place a dough ball on the board, dab with a little more melted butter, flatten slightly with your fingers, then stretch the dough outwards, working from the centre to the edge, until you have a circle of even thickness about 15cm (6in) in diameter. Repeat with the remaining dough balls, making them as thin as possible without tearing the pastry. Brush with a little beaten egg. Put a heaped tablespoon of stuffing on the bottom half of each dough circle in a half-moon shape, leaving a little lip at the bottom so they can be sealed. Fold over the top half of the dough to make half-moon parcels. Seal the parcels, making sure no air bubbles remain. Flute the edges of the dough using your thumb and forefinger.

4 Heat a heavy frying pan over a medium-high heat. Drop a couple of the roti parcels into the frying pan and fry for 2–3 minutes on each side until golden. Drain on kitchen paper. Continue frying in batches of 2 or 3 until all the parcels are cooked. Serve hot, accompanied by a bowl of the curry sauce on p48.

Roti prata, based on the legendary Indian flat bread, has near cult status in Singapore. People from all the island's cultures and nationalities enjoy this street food taste sensation. At the tiny café where I first enjoyed it I saw Malays, Indonesians, Chinese, and Indians, and I was not the only Westerner. It is often served with a bowl of curry sauce (see p48) or fresh coriander or coconut chutney. The bowl of the condiment is usually much bigger than the flat bread that you have to mop up the great sauce, so the only thing to do is to order another roti prata ...

Gulai ayam Creamy coconut curry sauce

Serves 6–8

2 garlic cloves, halved and any green inner shoot removed

4 fresh red chillies, deseeded and finely chopped

4 cm (1¾in) piece of fresh root ginger

10 whole macadamia nuts or cashew nuts

15 shallots or 3 onions, finely chopped

1 tablespoon coriander seeds

2 teaspoons cumin seeds

1 teaspoon fennel seeds

3cm (1¼in) piece of cinnamon stick

¼ teaspoon ground nutmeg

1 teaspoon ground turmeric

a little vegetable oil

400ml (14fl oz) coconut cream

juice of ½ lemon

salt and freshly ground black pepper

This curry sauce is the classic accompaniment to roti prata (see pp46–7). The use of coconut cream betrays its Malay and Singaporean roots. A great dipping sauce, it can also be used as the base for cooking anything from chicken or prawns to seasonal vegetables.

1 Using a pestle and mortar, pound the garlic, chilli, and ginger. Add the macadamia nuts and pound into a paste, before adding the shallot and working until smooth.

2 In a heavy frying pan over a medium-high heat, dry-roast the coriander seeds, cumin seeds, fennel seeds, and cinnamon stick for 1 minute. Add the nutmeg and turmeric, and cook for a further minute until aromatic. Remove the spices from the pan, and grind to a fine powder using a pestle and mortar, or a spice grinder.

3 Using the same pan, fry the shallot paste in a little oil over a medium-high heat for 3–4 minutes. Add the ground toasted spices, and continue frying for another 3 minutes. (If you are using this sauce for chicken, vegetables, or prawns, add them now and stir to coat with the spices.) Add the coconut cream and bring to the boil. Season well with salt and pepper. Reduce the heat, and simmer for 10 minutes until the sauce is thickened. Add the lemon juice and check the seasoning. Adjust to suit your taste if necessary. There should be a sweet richness from the coconut cream and macadamia nuts, while the spices and chilli will be hot. The lemon juice cuts the rich fattiness.

4 Transfer to a small serving bowl if using as a dipping sauce for roti prata (pp46–7). Serve warm or hot. (This sauce can be made in advance and reheated gently when needed.)

Sate sapi Indonesian beef sate skewers

Serves 6

1kg (2¼lb) beef rump, cut into
  2cm (1in) cubes

½ teaspoon ground turmeric

4 lime leaves, roughly chopped (if not
  available use grated zest of 1 lime)

2 stalks lemongrass

1 teaspoon sea salt

1 tablespoon tamarind pulp (see p30)

1 tablespoon plain flour

For the spice paste

1 tablespoon coriander seeds

1 teaspoon cumin seeds

1 teaspoon freshly ground black pepper

5 fresh red chillies, deseeded and
  finely chopped

3 garlic cloves, halved and any green
  inner shoot removed

4cm (1¾in) piece of fresh root ginger,
  finely chopped

4 shallots, finely chopped

1 teaspoon ground turmeric

a little vegetable oil

*There are many varieties
of sate, and they appear
in Thailand and Vietnam,
and throughout Singapore,
Malaysia, and Indonesia.
You can make sate using
chicken, beef, or pork.
This delicious version is
included because it is quite
different from how many
people usually perceive sate.*

1 You will need about 25 bamboo skewers. Soak them in cold water for at
least an hour before threading the beef onto them, so that they do not burn.

2 Put the beef in a large glass or ceramic dish. Combine the turmeric, lime
leaf, lemongrass, salt, and tamarind pulp. Use it to coat the beef, and
marinate in the refrigerator for at least 4 hours or preferably overnight.

3 Dry-roast the coriander and cumin seeds in a small frying pan over a
medium-high heat for 2 minutes until aromatic. Using a pestle and mortar,
grind into a fine powder, then add the pepper and chilli. Continue to work until
smooth, adding the garlic, ginger, shallot, and turmeric in turn. Add a splash of
water to make a smooth paste. Heat a little vegetable oil in a wok over a
medium-high heat, and stir-fry the paste for 4 minutes or so until fragrant.

4 Add the beef to the wok with the paste, reserving the marinade liquid. Add
300ml (10fl oz) water and simmer for 4–5 minutes. Remove the beef and
carefully thread onto the skewers. Heat a char-grill or ridged cast-iron grill pan
until hot. Grill the beef skewers for 2–3 minutes on each side. Mix the flour with
1 tablespoon of the reserved marinade to make a paste, then add to a saucepan
with the remaining marinade. Bring to the boil over a medium heat, and stir
continuously until thickened. Serve the beef skewers with the hot dipping sauce.

Nonya sambal
Spicy green vegetable stir-fry

sambals are often fiery hot side dishes that are used much like a condiment to accompany other dishes. The sambal oelek used here is an Indonesian speciality. There are many different types and styles, and they appeal to all ethnic groups in Malaysia, singapore, and Indonesia. On the hawker stalls in singapore and Malaysia, you will find regional varieties using lots of different seasonal vegetables. Experiment with other green vegetables such as asparagus, green beans, and broccoli. When this dish is part of a larger selection of dishes it helps to create a truly southeast Asian feel.

Serves 4–6

1 head of choy sum (Chinese flowering cabbage) or 500g (1lb 2oz) purple sprouting broccoli

2 heads of pak choy or bok choy

1 tablespoon vegetable oil

3 garlic cloves, crushed

4cm (1¾in) piece of fresh root ginger, grated

125g (4½oz) green beans, topped and tailed

20g (¾oz) bean sprouts, rinsed

handful of fresh mint leaves

handful of fresh coriander leaves

salt and freshly ground black pepper

For the sauce

1 tablespoon sambal oelek

1 tablespoon sweet soy sauce

1 tablespoon light soy sauce

1 tablespoon honey

1 tablespoon hoisin sauce

1 Cut the stems of the choy sum into 4cm (1¾in) lengths and separate the leaves. Cut the pak choy in half lengthways, then cut each half into 4 wedges through the base.

2 To make the sauce, combine all the ingredients in a small saucepan, and reduce over a high heat for 2 minutes. Remove from the heat.

3 Heat a wok over a medium-high heat and add the oil. Stir-fry the garlic and ginger for about 30 seconds until golden brown and fragrant. Add the choy sum stems, pak choy, green beans, reduced sauce, and 1 tablespoon water, and stir-fry for 2 minutes. Next add the choy sum leaves and stir-fry for a further minute or until tender. Tip in the sprouts, mint, and coriander, and toss through for 30 seconds until wilted.

4 Taste a little of the vegetables with the sauce and adjust the seasoning to taste. Season with salt and pepper. It should be hot and spicy, but with salty, sour, and sweet flavours present and in balance. Serve immediately.

Chee pow kai Paper-wrapped chicken

Makes 23–30 parcels

3cm (1¼in) piece of fresh root
  ginger, peeled

1 tablespoon light soy sauce

2 tablespoons rice wine

1 teaspoon spiced salt (see below)

½ teaspoon sugar

5 star anise, broken into pieces

vegetable oil for deep-frying

6 chicken breasts

freshly picked coriander leaves (optional)

fresh chilli sauce (optional)

freshly ground black pepper

For the spiced salt

2 tablespoons salt

1 teaspoon five-spice powder

These morsels make a great tasty snack and are fun to serve because each of your guests gets a small pile of packages containing tasty marinated chicken pieces. They could be served canapé-style to accompany drinks or on a buffet table as part of a wider selection. The packages' contents are intensely perfumed with star anise and ginger. You could also make them using cubes of fish or pork, or some prawns. Or perhaps you would like them more spicy, or with a different combination of spices.

1 To make the spiced salt, mix together the salt and five-spice powder. Dry-roast in a clean frying pan over a low heat for 3–4 minutes until fragrant, stirring the mixture to prevent it catching. This keeps indefinitely.

2 Using a pestle and mortar, crush the ginger until it is a rough pulp. Take the pulp in your hand and squeeze all the juice from the ginger into a bowl. (Alternatively, finely chop the ginger, then mash on a board using the back of a knife until you have a rough pulp.) Discard the squeezed pulp.

3 Mix the juice with the soy sauce, rice wine, spiced salt, sugar, star anise, and 1 tablespoon oil. Lay the chicken in a flat glass or ceramic dish. Pour the marinade over the top and season with pepper. Marinate the chicken in the refrigerator for at least 30 minutes.

4 Cut some greaseproof paper into 30 rectangles measuring about 30 x 15cm (12 x 6in) each. Lightly oil each piece of paper. Cut each chicken breast into 5 even-sized pieces, and place a piece of chicken on each piece of paper with a little piece of star anise picked from the marinade. Tightly wrap up the chicken like a small parcel, using toothpicks to secure the edges.

5 Heat the oil in a heavy pan over a medium-high heat for deep-frying. Fry the chicken parcels in batches for 3–4 minutes or until the paper browns. Drain well on kitchen paper and serve, allowing your guests to unwrap the parcels for themselves. Garnish with lots of freshly picked coriander and fresh chilli sauce (if using).

Chao wu xiang sen Sichuan-style vegetable stir-fry with Chinese chives

Serves 4–6

1 tablespoon vegetable oil

1 small Chinese cabbage or hard white cabbage, cut into equal-sized chunks about 4cm (1¾in) square

3 heads of baby bok choy, cut into equal-sized chunks about 4cm (1¾in) square

10 purple sprouting broccoli stalks, cut into 4cm (1¾in) lengths

10 fresh asparagus stalks, cut into 4cm (1¾in) lengths

2 tablespoons light soy sauce

6 spring onions, finely sliced

20g (¾oz) fresh bean sprouts

20 Chinese chives stems, snipped into 3 equal lengths

handful of fresh coriander leaves

salt and freshly ground black pepper

For the paste

grated zest of 2 limes

juice of 1 lime

4cm (1¾in) piece of fresh root ginger, grated

1 teaspoon five-spice powder

1 tablespoon sweet soy sauce

1 To make the paste, mix all the ingredients together in a bowl. Heat the oil in a wok over a medium-high heat. Add the cabbage, bok choy, broccoli, asparagus, and 1 tablespoon of the light soy sauce. Stir-fry for 1 minute. Add the paste, and continue to stir-fry for another 2 minutes until the vegetables are just tender.

2 Next add the remaining tablespoon light soy sauce with the spring onion, bean sprouts, and Chinese chives. Cook until wilted, then add the coriander leaves. Taste and check the seasoning, and adjust where appropriate. Serve immediately, alongside grilled fish or meat, and other Asian dishes.

Chinese five-spice powder works very well with soy sauce and cabbage, which might be served with barbecued beef, pork, or duck. The Sichuan pepper it contains has a brilliant tongue-tingling effect. Chinese chives or garlic chives are more strongly flavoured than the more common chives found in the supermarket. They are usually cooked to soften the strong flavours, and are particularly good in stir-fries. Chinese chives are available in Chinese and Asian food stores. If you can't find them, use a combination of spring onions and ordinary chives.

Cucur udang Singapore prawn fritters with sweet chilli sauce

Makes 12 fritters

200g (7oz) plain flour

½ teaspoon baking powder

¼ teaspoon ground turmeric

1 teaspoon sea salt

1 bunch of fresh chives, finely chopped

1 fresh red chilli, deseeded and
finely chopped

4 spring onions, finely sliced

100g (3½oz) fresh bean sprouts, rinsed
and drained well

500ml (16fl oz) vegetable oil for frying

24 fresh prawns, peeled and deveined

freshly picked coriander, to garnish

For the sweet chilli sauce

3 fresh red chillies, deseeded and
finely chopped

2 garlic cloves, finely chopped

1 tablespoon caster sugar

2 tablespoons white vinegar

juice of 1 lime

Prawn fritters and sweet chilli sauce make an almost inescapable pairing in Singaporean cuisine. And these definitely form the sort of moreish morsels that go down a treat. They work well as part of a buffet-style meal or as canapés for a party.

1 To make the fritters, sift the flour, baking powder, turmeric, and salt into a bowl. Whisk in 200ml (7fl oz) water to make a thick batter with the consistency of double cream. Add the chives, chilli, spring onion, and bean sprouts. Mix together well, and pour the batter into a jug.

2 Combine all the ingredients for the sweet chilli sauce. Add 4 tablespoons water, stir, and set aside.

3 Heat the oil in a heavy pan over a medium-high heat for deep-frying. Dip a small ladle into the hot oil and hold it there to heat for 15 seconds. Remove the ladle from the heat, allowing any excess oil to drip off. Half-fill the ladle with some of the batter, then press 2 prawns into the batter. Very carefully immerse the entire ladle with prawns into the hot oil (take extra care as the oil will spit because of the moisture in the fritters). Deep-fry for 2–3 minutes. Using a spatula or a small sharp knife, prise the fritter from the ladle, slip into the oil, and fry for a further 3 minutes or until golden brown. Repeat the process until all of the prawns have been used.

4 Serve hot and crispy with the sweet chilli sauce for dipping. Fresh coriander can be added to either or both the sauce and the fritters as a garnish.

This unique salad is great as an energy-filled healthy snack. It can also be made with vegetables such as carrots or sugarsnap peas, or with roast vegetables such as pumpkin or broccoli.

Rojak Mango, papaya, and pineapple salad

Serves 4–6

½ small cucumber

¼ fresh pineapple

1 firm unripe mango

1 firm unripe papaya

1 crisp acidic apple such as Granny Smith

2 spring onions, finely sliced

½ bunch of fresh mint, leaves torn

100g (3½oz) roasted blanched peanuts, coarsely crushed

For the dressing

2 tablespoons shrimp paste

3 fresh red chillies, deseeded and finely chopped

4cm (1¾in) piece of fresh root ginger, grated

1 tablespoon mashed tamarind pulp (see p30)

juice of 1 lime

5 tablespoons boiling water

2 tablespoons fish sauce

3 tablespoons caster sugar

1 First wrap the shrimp paste for the dressing in foil, and bake in a preheated 180°C (350°F/Gas 4) oven for 10 minutes until it becomes nuttier and drier, and aromatic rather than pungent.

2 To make the dressing, grind the chillies and ginger using a pestle and mortar. Mix with the roasted prawn paste and mash into a pulp. Add the mashed tamarind, lime juice, water, fish sauce, and sugar.

3 To make the salad, cut each fruit differently to ensure there are different textures and uneven pieces. Roll-cut the cucumber by cutting a chunk on a diagonal about 4cm (1¾in) long. Roll the cucumber 90 degrees, then cut another diagonal chunk. Continue cutting and rolling in this fashion, so that you have irregular diagonal chunks. Peel the pineapple, mango, and papaya. Dice the pineapple, cut wedges of mango and apple, and shred the papaya into ribbons using a vegetable peeler. Put in a large serving bowl, and add the spring onion and mint. Toss through gently. Scatter over half the peanuts and stir through.

4 Pour the dressing over the fruit and toss well. Serve in individual bowls, garnished with the remaining peanuts and mint leaves.

Cha gio Crispy chicken spring rolls

Serves 4

4 tablespoons fish sauce

2 tablespoons freshly squeezed lime juice

2 fresh red chillies, deseeded and
  finely chopped

1 teaspoon sugar

500ml (16fl oz) vegetable oil for cooking

200g (7oz) oyster mushrooms,
  roughly chopped

2 garlic cloves, finely chopped

2 onions, finely chopped

250g (9oz) minced chicken fillet

4 spring onions, finely chopped

2 eggs, beaten

4cm (1¾in) piece of fresh root
  ginger, grated

1 teaspoon five-spice powder

½ teaspoon salt

30 fresh coriander leaves, roughly chopped,
  plus 20 extra leaves, to serve

16 rice paper wrappers

2 tablespoons freshly squeezed lime juice

1 teaspoon sugar

20 fresh mint leaves, to serve

freshly ground black pepper

Vietnamese spring rolls are very delicate compared to other Asian varieties. They should be about the length of a man's index finger and only just a little wider. They are served with a dipping sauce and a bowlful of aromatic herbs such as coriander, mint, and Thai basil (which has a liquorice or aniseed flavour), as well as other lemony and peppery leaves. To eat, take the fried spring roll, wrap it in a couple of leaves, and dip it into the hot, salty, and sour dipping sauce, causing a culinary firework display in your mouth. The herbs provide a refreshing zing and crunch.

1 Make a dipping sauce by mixing together half the fish sauce, the lime juice, half the chilli, and the sugar in a small bowl. Add 3–4 tablespoons warm water and stir. Set aside. Heat a little oil in a heavy pan over a high heat. Add the mushroom and fry for 3–4 minutes until browned. Remove from the pan. Heat a little extra oil in the same pan and add the garlic. Reduce the heat and fry for another 2 minutes, then add the onion and cook for 8–10 minutes until softened. Chop the mushrooms into smaller pieces and return to the pan. Season well.

2 Mix the remaining fish sauce and chilli, chicken, spring onion, egg, ginger, five-spice powder, salt, and chopped coriander in a bowl. Add the mushroom mixture. Take a small piece of mixture and fry in the pan. Taste and adjust the seasoning – it should be well spiced with an underlying sweetness.

3 Soak the rice paper wrappers 4 at a time in warm water for about a minute. Lay on a clean damp cloth. Place a tablespoon of the filling on each one, about 3cm (1¼in) from the edge nearest to you. Fold in the two sides on each wrapper and roll tightly away from you, like a cigar. Heat a wok or heavy pan over a medium heat for a couple of minutes. Add the oil and heat. To test, carefully drop in a spring roll – it should sizzle and bubble. Reduce the heat by a third and fry the spring rolls for about 5 minutes in small batches. Drain and serve hot with the dipping sauce and whole coriander and mint leaves in the centre of the table.

Nua prik thai nahm jim

Skewers of beef with green chilli sauce

Serves 4–6

400g (14oz) tender beef such as rump steak, sirloin, or rib eye, trimmed of any fat or sinew

2 tablespoons light soy sauce

1 tablespoon vegetable oil

1 teaspoon caster sugar

3 coriander roots, cleaned and chopped (if not available, use the lower part of the stems, finely chopped)

1 tablespoon coriander seeds

pinch of salt

20 white peppercorns

3 slices fresh root ginger

2 stalks lemongrass, finely chopped

1 head of garlic (leave cloves unpeeled)

20–30 fresh coriander leaves, to garnish

freshly ground black pepper

For the green chilli sauce

3 fresh green chillies, deseeded and finely chopped

2 garlic cloves

2 coriander roots, rinsed and chopped

1 teaspoon salt

2 teaspoons caster sugar

30 fresh coriander leaves

juice of 3 limes

2 tablespoons fish sauce

I had these beef skewers in a Bangkok night market. They were so irresistible that, even though I was trying not to repeat myself, I got the taxi to stop there for another taste the next night when I was on my way to the airport. The use of white pepper here means that the recipe is an old Siamese one. White pepper was used in Southeast Asia for many centuries, to provide heat for the spicy food. It was only after the Spanish and Portuguese went to South America in the 16th century that hot chillies were transported around the world to countries such as Thailand.

1 Soak some bamboo skewers in cold water. Cut the beef into 2–3 cm (¾–1¼in) cubes. Mix together the light soy sauce, oil, caster sugar, and some black pepper. Use this to marinate the beef in the refrigerator for at least 4 hours.

2 Crush the coriander root, coriander seeds, salt, and peppercorns using a pestle and mortar, or in a food processor. Add the ginger, lemongrass, and garlic; continue to pound or process until a rough coarse-ground paste. Rub all over the meat. Heat a griddle pan for at least 5 minutes until really hot. Skewer 3 or 4 pieces of meat onto each of the skewers. In batches, grill for 3 minutes or until golden brown on one side. (Don't move the meat while it is cooking.) Turn over and cook for a further 2 minutes until crisp on the outside and medium rare inside. Remove from the pan and rest for a few minutes. Garnish with coriander.

3 Make the green chilli sauce. Using a pestle and mortar, crush the green chillies, garlic, and coriander root with the salt and sugar until smooth. Add the coriander leaves and keep pounding until a green paste. Add the lime juice and fish sauce. Check the seasoning. If it is very acidic, dilute with a little water. Serve as a dipping sauce to accompany the hot skewers.

Caro do bien

South Vietnamese seafood curry

Serves 4

1 tablespoon vegetable oil	400ml (14fl oz) coconut cream
4 shallots, finely chopped	5 fresh lime leaves or finely grated
3 garlic cloves, finely chopped	zest of 4 limes
2 stalks lemongrass, tough outer leaves	250g (9oz) peeled raw tiger prawns
discarded, finely sliced	350g (12oz) firm white fish such as
30g (1oz) fresh root ginger, finely grated	snapper or bream, skinned and cut into
½ teaspoon hot crushed dried red chilli	3cm (1¼in) cubes
1 teaspoon mild curry powder	20 fresh Thai basil leaves, roughly chopped
½ teaspoon ground cinnamon	30 fresh coriander leaves, roughly chopped
½ teaspoon ground star anise	6 spring onions, finely chopped
½ teaspoon ground coriander	juice of 1 lime
2 fresh red chillies, deseeded and	2 tablespoons fish sauce
finely chopped	

1 Cook this in a well-ventilated space because of the aromatic fumes from the spices and the chilli. Heat the oil in a wok or high-sided heavy pan over a medium-high heat. Add the shallot, garlic, half the lemongrass, and half the ginger. Fry for 3–4 minutes. Add the dried spices and half the fresh chilli. Fry for a further 2–3 minutes until very aromatic. This mixture forms the curry base.

2 Pour in the coconut cream and 300ml (10fl oz) water. Add 3 of the lime leaves and bring to a gentle boil. Continue boiling gently until reduced by half. When reduced, add the prawns and fish. Reduce the heat, and gently simmer for 5 minutes (the fish is very delicate). When the fish is poached, add the Thai basil, coriander, and spring onion.

3 Take the remaining lime leaves and trim away the stems with a sharp knife, cutting away from you. Roll the two leaves together like a cigar and finely slice. Garnish the curry with the remaining lemongrass, red chilli, and ginger, and the shredded lime leaves. Drizzle over the lime juice and fish sauce. Serve with lots of rice or rice noodles, as a standalone dish or as part of a larger spread of dishes. It works very well served as a small portion in quite a smart setting like a drinks party. This gives guests a great taster and still allows room for more.

Vietnam has nearly two thousand miles of coast, and huge river deltas – the Mekong, the Perfume River, and the Red River. Fish, shellfish, and anything that swims or lives near water are an essential part of Vietnamese life and make up a large percentage of the Vietnamese diet. This rustic fisherman's stew has a depth of complex flavours. You can use any combination of fish and shellfish. You could also make a vegetarian curry by substituting the fish with fresh seasonal vegetables of your choice.

Char siew Chinese barbecue pork

Char siew is deliciously simple to make. It is often eaten as a snack and is available anywhere there is a Chinese culinary influence. It can be eaten on its own or with some crisp lettuce and slices of cucumber. You can even use it as a component of another dish such as a stir-fry or a noodle dish or a soup, all of which are available from stalls in places such as Singapore, Malaysia, and Vietnam.

Serves 4–6

3 tablespoons fish sauce

½ tablespoon dark soy sauce

1 tablespoon sugar

1 tablespoon rice wine

1 teaspoon five-spice powder

600g (1lb 5oz) fresh pork shoulder, cut into
  long strips 3–4 cm (1¼–1¾in) thick

1 Combine all the ingredients except the pork to make a marinade. Stir well to mix. Place the pork in a glass or ceramic dish, pour over the marinade, and leave in the refrigerator, covered, for at least 2 hours. Turn a few times to ensure that the meat is coated by the marinade.

2 Heat your barbecue to medium, and place the pork on the grill where the heat is not too fierce. (You can also cook this in a griddle pan or under an overhead grill.) Cook the pork for 15 minutes, brushing regularly with excess marinade and turning to avoid it burning. Serve hot or cold, in salads, soups, or stir-fries, or with some chilli jam or sambal-style sauce.

Goi du du Hot and sour squid and green mango salad

Serves 4–6

300g (10oz) baby squid, cleaned and
    cut in half lengthways

2 unripe green mangos

1 green unripe papaya

3cm (1¼in) piece of fresh root ginger

5 lime leaves (if not available, use grated
    zest of 3 limes), finely sliced

4 spring onions, finely sliced

2 fresh green chillies, deseeded and
    finely sliced

2 stalks lemongrass, tough outer
    leaves discarded, finely sliced

20 fresh mint leaves, roughly chopped

handful of fresh coriander leaves,
    roughly chopped

50g (1¾oz) blanched peanuts or cashew
    nuts or sesame seeds, or a combination
    of all three), dry-roasted until golden

salt and freshly ground black pepper

For the dressing

1 tablespoon tamarind paste (see p30)

2 tablespoons fish sauce

1 tablespoon light soy sauce

juice of 2 limes

juice of 1 orange

1 teaspoon palm sugar or caster sugar

1   If the squid is thick, turn over so the outer side is facing upwards. With a knife, score diagonal lines from corner to corner two-thirds of the way into the flesh. Repeat in the opposite direction so that you have a diamond pattern. Heat a char-grill or griddle pan until very hot. Season the squid with salt and pepper, and place skin-side down on the grill pan. Leave for 90 seconds, then turn over. Cook for the same amount of time on the other side. When it curls up, it is ready. Place the squid on a board, and cut into bite-sized pieces.

2   Peel the green mango and papaya. Still using a vegetable peeler, shave slices of the flesh, stack in piles of 5 shavings, and finely chop, resulting in matchstick-like battens. Put the mango, papaya, and squid in a large bowl. Finely slice the ginger into thin shavings, then cut into matchsticks or grate. Add the ginger, lime leaf, spring onion, chilli, and lemongrass to the bowl with the squid. Sprinkle in two-thirds of the mint, coriander, and nuts. Toss through.

3   Combine all the ingredients for the dressing. Pour over the salad, tossing gently to mix. Check the seasoning – it should be sour and hot, slightly salty, and sweet. Serve sprinkled with the remaining mint, coriander, and nuts.

Green unripe mango and papaya are used to spectacular effect all over Southeast Asia. They are used like a vegetable, providing a crisp sour quality. If they are not available, use a combination of shredded cucumber, crisp lettuce, and some crisp acidic apple cut into thin slices. Variations of this salad are available from all manner of stalls and cafés in Vietnam, Thailand, Cambodia, Laos, Northern Malaysia, and Singapore. You can also make it with prawns, scallops, or grilled white fish, or perhaps pork, beef, or chicken instead.

Penang laksa Seafood laksa

Serves 4–6

4cm (1¾in) fresh root ginger, grated

2 tablespoons tamarind pulp (see p30)

1 teaspoon sea salt

500g (1lb 2 oz) red snapper, skinned

4 dried chillies, crushed

2 stalks lemongrass, outer layer removed

2 fresh red chillies, deseeded and
    finely chopped

8 shallots, peeled

2 tablespoons shrimp paste, roasted
    (see p58)

150g (5½ oz) dried rice noodles,
    about 5mm (¼in) wide

200g (7oz) fresh crabmeat

200g (7oz) peeled and deveined
    fresh prawns

juice of 2 limes

15 Thai basil leaves

½ cucumber, cut into matchsticks

200g (7oz) fresh pineapple,
    cut into matchsticks

handful of fresh mint leaves

Penang is a small island off the coast of Malaysia near the border with southern Thailand. Despite its diminutive size, it has had a large culinary influence within Asia. The region is famed for its fiery hot curries and spectacular seafood dishes. There are many regional variations of the famous laksa soup; this one was one of my favourites.

1 Put the ginger, 1 tablespoon of the tamarind pulp, and salt into a pan. Cover with 1 litre (1¾ pints) water and bring to the boil. Reduce the heat and add the fish. Cover and simmer for 6–8 minutes. Remove from the heat. Extract the fish and leave to cool. (Do not discard the cooking liquor.) Once cool, discard any bones and set the fish aside. Strain the cooking liquor – this forms the stock.

2 Meanwhile, soak the dried chillies in a little boiling water for 10 minutes until soft, then remove and discard the seeds. Soak the seedless chillies in a fresh batch of hot water for another 10 minutes. Drain and finely chop. Finely slice the lemongrass. Process the lemongrass and dried and fresh chillies to a paste. Add 6 of the shallots, the roast shrimp paste, and a little fish stock. Work until very smooth. Put into a saucepan and cover with the rest of the fish stock. Bring to the boil and cook uncovered for 20 minutes, then reduce to a simmer.

3 Soak the rice noodles in warm water for 5 minutes. Bring another pan of water to the boil, drain the noodles, and cook in the boiling water for 3 minutes. Drain, and run the noodles under cold water to remove excess starch.

4 Return the fish to the simmering stock, add the crabmeat and prawns, and simmer for 3 minutes. Add the remaining tablespoon of tamarind pulp, the lime juice, and the basil. Check the seasoning. Serve in bowls with the noodles at the bottom and the fish and broth poured over. Garnish each bowl with cucumber, pineapple, mint, and the remaining shallots cut into slivers.

Nua nam tok Hot and sour grilled beef salad with roasted rice

In Thailand and Vietnam, there are many variations of hot and sour salads. The dressing is what sets this salad apart, with its pungent mixture of hot red chilli, shredded ginger, and lime juice. In an authentic Southeast Asian meal there are numerous courses, arriving at the table in a continuous stream. From the middle of the meal onwards, there may be any number of dishes being eaten together. A salad such as this comes in the first half of the meal. For a vegetarian alternative, try grilled mushrooms and asparagus in place of beef.

Serves 4

400g (14oz) topside of beef

1 teaspoon ground cinnamon

1 teaspoon ground cumin

1 teaspoon five-spice powder

2 fresh red chillies, deseeded and
  finely chopped

4cm (1¾in) piece of fresh root ginger,
  finely sliced into thin matchsticks

4 spring onions, cut into fine slivers

2 shallots, finely sliced

½ bunch of fresh coriander, leaves picked

20 fresh mint leaves

juice of 3 limes

1 tablespoon fish sauce

2 tablespoons light soy sauce

4 tablespoons ground roasted
  rice (see below)

salt and freshly ground black pepper

1 Season the meat with the cinnamon, cumin, five-spice powder, salt, and black pepper. On a preheated grill or griddle pan, cook the beef over a medium-high heat for 6–8 minutes until medium rare. Rest the meat in a warm place for 5 minutes.

2 To make the salad, slice the beef and mix in a bowl with the chilli, ginger, spring onion, and shallot. Sprinkle over the coriander and half the mint. Add the lime juice, fish sauce, and soy sauce. Add half of the ground roasted rice and save the other half for garnishing. Toss gently. The flavours should be hot, sour, and salty. Add more chillies, lime juice, and fish sauce if necessary.

3 Shred the remaining mint. Serve the salad garnished with the remaining roasted rice and the mint.

Roasted rice Roasted rice is not difficult to make and has a great nutty flavour. It is similar to toasted sesame seeds, so you could use these instead if you like. But it is worth making the effort. Simply scatter a couple of handfuls of raw jasmine or sticky rice on an oven tray. Bake in a preheated 180°C (350°C/Gas 4) oven for 6–8 minutes or until evenly golden and fragrant. Check regularly while cooking to avoid scorching. Remove from the oven and allow to cool on the tray. When cool, grind using a pestle and mortar. It is very hard, so it needs to be pounded, until it is broken up into fine pieces but not ground to a powder.

Banh tom Hanoi prawn cakes

Makes 20 cakes

125g (4½oz) plain flour, sifted

85g (3oz) rice flour

½ teaspoon salt

½ teaspoon baking powder

1 teaspoon sugar

150g (5oz) sweet potato

3 spring onions, thinly sliced

250g (9oz) fresh prawns, peeled, deveined,
    and cut into 1cm (½in) pieces

vegetable oil for frying

freshly ground black pepper

1 lime, cut into quarters

½ cucumber, thinly sliced

handful of bean sprouts

¼ crisp lettuce such as iceberg

5 sprigs of fresh mint

5 sprigs of fresh coriander

5 sprigs of Thai basil

some rocket or watercress

Nuac cham dipping sauce

3 small fresh bird's-eye chillies, deseeded
    and thinly sliced

1 garlic clove, finely chopped

1 tablespoon sugar

juice of 2 limes

4 tablespoons fish sauce

1 To make the prawn cakes, mix the two types of flour with the salt, baking powder, sugar, and black pepper in a bowl. Stir in 220ml (7½fl oz) water until you have a smooth batter. Leave to rest for 10 minutes. Peel and cut the sweet potato into matchsticks. Add to the batter with the spring onion and prawns.

2 Make the dipping sauce using a pestle and mortar. Crush two-thirds of the chilli with the garlic and sugar until smooth. Add 100ml (3½ fl oz) warm water. Transfer to a bowl, and add the lime juice and fish sauce. Stir to dissolve the sugar. Sprinkle in the remaining chilli and set aside.

3 Heat vegetable oil to a depth of 2–3cm (¾–1¼in) in a heavy pan. When the oil is shimmering, test to see whether it is hot enough. Drop in a little of the batter. It should bubble and sizzle straight away. Taste and adjust seasoning.

4 Place 2 heaped tablespoons of the prawn batter onto a metal spatula. Pat into an irregular shape about 1cm (½in) thick. Push the prawn cake into the oil using a metal spoon. Cook in batches of 3 or 4 at a time, turning once until golden brown on all sides. Drain on kitchen paper and keep warm. To eat, put the lime, cucumber, sprouts, lettuce, herbs, and rocket in the centre of the table. Wrap a prawn cake in some fresh greens and lettuce, then dip into the sauce.

In the centre of Hanoi there is a series of lakes, with ancient pagodas and monuments that are captivating at any time of the day. At 5.30 in the morning, the lakeshore is packed with Hanoi residents doing tai chi and other morning exercises. At the weekend, the lakes are a popular destination with families who come to admire the pagodas at sunset and eat banh tom. I counted about ten outside cafés that were selling exactly the same prawn cakes to the many passers-by, in the same way that a fairground has lots of stalls all selling toffee apples.

Ayam golek Spiced grilled chicken with coconut cream

Malaysian food has an intense depth of flavour that comes from use of fresh aromatic spices such as lemongrass, ginger, and galangal. It is delicious and, once tried, it soon becomes a firm favourite. The spice mixture and method of cooking here are very versatile. You could make it with a large whole chicken to be enjoyed by a number of people, instead of allowing one small baby chicken or poussin per person as here. Or it could be made with skewers of chicken marinated for a longer time and quickly grilled to ensure a delicious succulent snack.

Serves 4

4 dried chillies, soaked in hot
 water to soften
5 shallots, roughly chopped
2 garlic cloves
2cm (¾in) piece of fresh root ginger
2cm (¾in) piece of galangal (if galangal
 is not available, use double the
 quantity of ginger)

1 teaspoon salt
4 stalks lemongrass, tough outer
 leaves discarded
4 baby chickens (poussins)
300ml (10fl oz) coconut cream
2 teaspoons sugar
juice of 2 limes

1 This chicken dish can be started on the barbecue or in a griddle pan, then finished in the oven. Preheat the oven to 200°C (400°F/Gas 6).

2 Drain the dried chillies once soft, and blend or process with the shallot, garlic, ginger, galangal, and salt. Add a little water to form a paste. Work the hardest ingredients first, then the softer ones, to ensure the paste is very smooth.

3 Bruise the lemongrass using the back of a heavy knife. Stuff each chicken with the lemongrass, then rub the spice paste both inside and out. Put the remaining spice mixture in a pan with the coconut cream and sugar. Simmer until reduced by half.

4 Place the baby chickens on the hot barbecue or griddle, and grill for 3–4 minutes on all sides. Transfer to an oven tray, and roast in the oven for 15 minutes or so, basting the chicken with the coconut mixture every 5 minutes or so while it is cooking, until the chicken is tender and the coconut spice mixture is all used up. (If you are cooking a large chicken, it will need to be roasted in the oven for about 45 minutes after you have grilled it on all sides.)

5 Before serving, pour all the juices from the pan over the chicken and finish with the lime juice. This marinade and method of cooking is also suitable for drumsticks or chicken pieces. Serve accompanied by rice, fresh salad, vegetables, or a Singapore rojak salad (see pp58–9).

Goi bun Salad of roast pork with cucumber and sesame seeds

This Vietnamese salad works particularly well if some of the ingredients are still warm, such as the pork and the dressing, or the sesame seeds. There is a brilliant contrast between different textures, as well as flavours. The dressing provides heat from the chilli; the fish and soy sauces provide the salt; and the vinegar, lime juice, and lemongrass provide the sour. All these flavours work very well with the crisp textures of the cucumber and celery.

Serves 4

500g (1lb 2oz) pork tenderloin

50g (1¾oz) sesame seeds

2 small cucumbers, halved
  lengthways and deseeded

1 head of celery, white central part only

3 spring onions, finely sliced

1 fresh red chilli, deseeded and
  finely chopped

grated zest of 1 lime

2 stalks lemongrass, tough outer leaves
  discarded, finely sliced

30 fresh coriander leaves, torn

20 fresh mint leaves, torn

salt and freshly ground black pepper

For the dressing

2 teaspoons sugar

juice of 2 limes

2 tablespoons rice vinegar

4 coriander roots, roughly chopped

1 fresh red chilli, deseeded and
  roughly chopped

2 tablespoons toasted sesame oil

1 tablespoon fish sauce

1 tablespoon light soy sauce

1 Preheat the oven to 200°C (400°F/Gas 6). Season the pork on all sides with salt and pepper. Heat a chargrill or griddle pan over a medium-high heat. Grill the pork on all sides, then transfer to a baking tray. Roast in the oven for 10–12 minutes or until cooked through. Allow to rest for 10 minutes, keeping warm. While the pork is roasting, dry-roast the sesame seeds in the oven until pale golden brown. Watch carefully to make sure they don't scorch. Set aside.

2 To make the dressing, put the sugar, lime juice, and vinegar in a small saucepan. Add 3 teaspoons water and bring to the boil. Add the coriander root and chilli, and stir through. Pour the liquid into a food processor and pulse until completely smooth. Stir in the sesame oil, fish sauce, and soy sauce.

3 Cut the cucumber into 4cm (1¾in) chunks, then into matchsticks. Cut the celery in the same way. Put the cucumber and celery in a large bowl. Add the spring onion, chilli, lime zest, lemongrass, and most of the sesame seeds. Sprinkle in the coriander and mint, reserving some for the garnish. Cut the pork into thin slices against the grain of the meat. Add to the rest of the salad. When ready to serve, pour the dressing over the salad and toss through. Garnish with the remaining coriander and mint, and sprinkle the sesame seeds over the top.

Kueh pisang
Banana and cinnamon pancakes

Makes 12 pancakes

250g (9oz) plain flour	6 large ripe bananas
1 teaspoon baking powder	2 tablespoons caster sugar
2 teaspoons ground cinnamon plus	pinch of salt
extra, to serve	vegetable oil for cooking
2 eggs, beaten	icing sugar, to serve
120ml (4fl oz) milk	freshly squeezed lemon juice, to serve

1 Sift the flour, baking powder, and the 2 teaspoons cinnamon into a large bowl. Make a well in the centre. Add the eggs and half the milk. Beat well until you have a smooth batter, then add the remaining milk and stir in thoroughly.

2 Peel the bananas and, using a fork, mash with the caster sugar and salt. Mix the mashed banana into the batter.

3 Sprinkle some greaseproof paper with a dusting of icing sugar to have ready when the pancakes are cooked. Heat a little oil in a frying pan over a medium-high heat. Tip out any excess oil, then drop in a dollop of the batter to make a pancake 12–18cm (5–7in) in diameter. (Alternatively, you can make smaller pancakes about the size of drop scones.) Fry on both sides until golden, flipping over with a spatula or egg slice about halfway through. Continue until all the batter has been used, turning the pancakes onto the icing sugar as you go.

4 Sprinkle each pancake with a little extra icing sugar and a pinch of extra ground cinnamon. Add a squeeze of lemon, fold each pancake into quarters, and serve hot.

No collection of hawker stalls or night market in Singapore or anywhere in Malaysia or Thailand would be complete without a stall selling some form of banana pancake, whether made with flour and milk, or with glutinous rice. Banana pancakes are the perfect end to a delicious meal of sate, fish cakes, and stir-fries that are all packed with flavours and fiery chillies. When strong flavours and chillies have bombarded your tongue, your taste buds recognize only sugar. This is why many southeast Asian desserts seem so very sweet when taken out of context.

Latin America and the Caribbean

The food styles and ingredients of Latin America are as vast and varied as the region. Ingredients such as members of the squash family, including pumpkin and courgette, have been grown for thousands of years. Chilli and corn cultivation date back just as far. In the Andes, early farmers grew peanuts, potatoes, and sweet potatoes 6,000 years ago. Before the Portuguese and Spanish travelled to the Americas in the 16th century, this bounteous larder remained untouched by the rest of the world. Yet, without it, we would not have corn, beans, potatoes, tomatoes, chillies, pumpkin, avocados, chocolate, to name but a few.

Day 23: Mexico City, Mexico Unfortunately, I had only a day to spend in Mexico's capital, as I was heading further south to Puebla, then on to the coast. Faced with this enormous, overwhelming city and limited time to discover as much about the food as possible, I decided that there was only one way forward. My plan was to try as many different dishes, taste combinations, and ingredients as possible. In just over 24 hours, I barely slept, instead opting to eat on average every 30–45 minutes. So much of it was so delicious that I wanted to finish everything that had been put in front of me. This soon became impossible, but undaunted I pressed on. After many hours, stall holders had begun to look at me in despair. I am sure they were wondering exactly who this guy was who ordered enough food for three or four people, sat there tasting, and writing notes, then tipped heavily and left, to be seen crossing the road and taking a stool at the next stall. Mexico as a whole is famed for its street food, and it is hugely popular with all manner of residents; businessmen and bankers can be seen eating alongside manual workers and students. Good food is essential to Mexicans, and there is enormous variety because virtually everything is available in one form or another from a street stall, café, or market. Some recipes have remained unchanged for hundreds and in some cases thousands of years.

Day 31: Salvador de Bahia, Brazil With so many cultures coexisting in Brazil, the food cannot help but be influenced by Brazil's ethnic diversity, although each region's cuisine remains quite loyally distinct. In Salvador de Bahia, the food and the culture are dominated by the heritage of its many African inhabitants, descendants of the thousands of slaves brought to Brazil by the Portuguese to work the plantations. In fact, the state of Bahia has the largest African population outside of the African continent. Here, every side dish, street food snack, or piece of grilled fish is served with a fiery chilli salsa made with coriander, tomato, onion, and vinegar – and, of course, the hot little pods themselves. I've always been completely addicted to chilli. I asked my wife on our first date if she liked it because I honestly didn't think I could go out with someone who didn't. Luckily for us both, she does! In Salvador de Bahia, however, even I had to proceed with caution. I came across a lethal little round purple chilli in a market. When I nibbled it – much to the amusement of the stall holder – it made my face go numb and I thought all of my teeth were going to fall out.

RICO MO
CON HUE
VASO CHICO Y JUGO
$300. MEDIANO
$400.

Caldo de sururu Spicy mussel soup

Serves 4–6

2 small fresh very hot red chillies, deseeded
  and finely chopped

2 garlic cloves

6 fresh coriander sprigs, leaves picked and
  stems finely chopped

2 tablespoons olive oil

2 medium white onions, finely chopped

2kg (4½lb) mussels in their shells

6 ripe tomatoes, roughly chopped

2 bay leaves

300ml (10fl oz) coconut cream

juice of 2 limes plus extra limes, cut into
  wedges, to garnish

sea salt and freshly ground black pepper

In the northeast of Brazil, in the state of Bahia, mussels are known as "sururu". This is a great soup to serve at the beginning of a meal. In Brazil it is served in small cups or shot glasses, and in many little cafés it can be found served alongside a cold glass of beer. For a crunchy addition, chopped roasted peanuts can be mixed through the soup.

1 Using a mortar and pestle, crush the chilli with the garlic and salt. Add the coriander stems and work into a paste. Heat a large heavy pan over a medium-high heat. Fry the chilli paste in the oil. Add the onion and cook for 3 minutes or so until softened. Tap each mussel lightly on the work surface, and discard any that do not open, then add the mussels, tomato, and 500ml (16fl oz) water to the onion mixture. Cover and cook for 3 minutes. Add the bay leaves and continue cooking until the mussels open (discard any unopened mussels). Remove from the heat, and transfer the mussels and onion to a bowl. Leave to cool. Strain the cooking liquor through a sieve and set aside.

2 Prise open the mussels completely; remove the meat and discard the shells. Put two-thirds of the mussel meat in a food processor with the cooled tomato and onion mixture. Purée with the coconut cream until smooth. Return the purée to the heavy pan with the strained mussel cooking liquor and another 500ml (16fl oz) water, bring to the boil, then reduce the heat and simmer for 10 minutes. Add the reserved whole mussels to the pan, season well with salt and pepper, and add the lime juice.

3 Taste the soup. It should be rich and creamy, with a good base of chilli. The lime juice cuts through the richness to ensure the soup has a perfect balance of flavours, rather than being cloying. Serve hot in small cups or shot glasses, with each serving garnished with a lime wedge.

Queijo na brasa Grilled salty cheese marinated with oregano

Makes 12 skewers

2 small dried red chillies, crushed

1 tablespoon dried oregano or
marjoram, crumbled

3 tablespoons olive oil

juice of ½ lemon

500g (1lb 2oz) *queijo de coalho* or haloumi
cheese, cut into 12 rectangular blocks

freshly ground black pepper

1 Crush the chilli with half the oregano, and mix with the olive oil and lemon
juice. Set aside.

2 Thread the cheese onto 12 bamboo skewers, and soak the cheese,
skewers and all, in cold water for an hour, to prevent the skewers burning
on the grill and to remove excess salt from the cheese.

3 Heat a charcoal barbecue until the coals are white hot. (If you want to
cook inside, heat a griddle pan until very hot.) When your barbecue or
griddle is ready, sprinkle the cheese skewers with the remaining oregano and
grindings of black pepper. Grill the cheese for 2–3 minutes on each side until
golden brown but still firm (not completely melted).

4 Arrange on a plate and pour over the olive oil dressing. Serve immediately.
These skewers are delicious as a snack or could be eaten at the start of a
summer barbecue before more dishes arrive. They work very well for meat eaters
and vegetarians alike because they are quite substantial and make a change
from grilled corn on the cob.

In Bahia, street food can easily be redefined as beach food. There are scores of little cafés and stalls where things are freshly made for lounging customers. Teenage boys and girls run around taking orders up and down the white sandy beach and ferrying them back to the cafés. There are also vendors who walk along selling their wares. It was from one of these that I had these fantastic skewers, fresh from a charcoal-filled brazier. When the smoky grilled cheese is handed over, it comes with a wad of paper towels and a warning in Portuguese that it is very hot. I take heed.

Acaraje com salada fresca Bean patties with avocado and tomato salad

These bean patties are extremely tasty, especially in combination with their usual accompaniment of salt-dried prawns and a zingy fresh salad. Street vendors often serve the acaraje split and filled with a prawn purée known as "vatapá", or in a vegetarian version with a tomato and chilli salsa, and they are traditionally cooked in palm oil. Stalls selling acaraje are found everywhere in Salvador de Bahia. Acaraje is an evening dish, enjoyed before you go on to a party – something at which the Brazilians excel.

Serves 4–6

For the acaraje

1kg (2¼lb) dried black-eyed beans
300g (10oz) onion, grated
1 teaspoon cayenne pepper
2 garlic cloves, finely chopped
4cm (1¾in) piece of fresh
   root ginger, grated
1 fresh hot red chilli, deseeded and
   finely chopped
vegetable oil for frying
sea salt and freshly ground black pepper

For the salad

1 avocado, sliced
4 ripe tomatoes, sliced
4 spring onions, sliced
2 fresh green chillies, deseeded and
   finely chopped
juice of 1 lemon
1 tablespoon vinegar
2 tablespoons good-quality olive oil

1 Soak the beans in cold water for 2 hours. Rinse well in fresh cold water, and remove the husks and black eyes. Put the beans and onion in a pan. Cover with water, bring to the boil, and simmer for about 40 minutes until soft. Drain. Purée the bean mixture and cayenne pepper in a food processor until smooth.

2 Heat a little oil in a heavy frying pan. Gently fry the garlic and ginger for 2 minutes until fragrant. Add the bean paste, season with salt and pepper, and keep over a low heat. Beat the mixture well with a wooden spoon to avoid it catching, as you would polenta. Cook for 15–20 minutes, stirring from the bottom occasionally. Check seasoning. Remove from the heat and set aside.

3 Heat oil in a heavy pan over a medium-high heat. When hot, take a dessertspoon and quickly dip it into the hot oil. Fill the spoon with bean mixture, forming a firm, round shape. Place in the hot oil. Continue until you have a few patties in the pan. Fry for 6–8 minutes until golden brown. Drain on kitchen paper. Keep cooking in small batches until all the mixture is used.

4 To make the salad, put the avocado, tomato, spring onion, and chilli in a bowl and mix together. Combine the lemon juice, vinegar, and olive oil. Season well with salt and pepper. Pour this dressing over the salad, and serve with the fried acaraje and perhaps some grilled prawns.

Barbecue jerk chicken with pineapple salsa

Serves 4

4 chicken breasts

4 tablespoons jerk paste (see below)

For the jerk paste

5 jalapeño chillies, deseeded and
  finely chopped

2 tablespoons ground allspice

1 tablespoon ground cinnamon

1 tablespoon ground nutmeg

juice of 3 limes

1 onion, finely chopped

grated zest of 2 oranges

½ tablespoon tamarind paste (see p30)

For the pineapple salsa

¼ fresh pineapple, peeled and
  cut into 1cm (½in) dice

1 crisp green apple, diced

½ bunch of fresh coriander

1 fresh red chilli, deseeded
  and diced

juice of 2 limes

1 small red onion, diced

pinch of sea salt

freshly ground black pepper

1 To make the jerk paste, blend or process all the paste ingredients to a purée. (This paste will keep for 5–7 days stored in a tightly sealed glass jar in the refrigerator.) Coat the chicken breasts with the jerk paste, and marinate in the refrigerator for at least 3–4 hours, preferably overnight.

2 When you are ready to cook, prepare the pineapple salsa by combining all the ingredients. Set aside until ready to use.

3 Heat the barbecue until hot. When it is the correct temperature, grill the meat on both sides until tender, and serve it with either the pineapple salsa or perhaps the peach salsa on pp94–5.

In Jamaica, jerk paste is traditionally used to marinate barbecue chicken or pork. The recipe here uses chicken breast, but chicken pieces such as drumsticks and thighs work just as well, as do pork ribs. The secret to success is in the marinating: the longer the better. The blend of spices is so invigorating to the taste buds it's quite addictive – no fingers in the jar now! The smell of the meat when it is cooking is evocative of the finished product. When it is done, it will be snapped up. The pineapple salsa supplies a fresh, zingy flavour that complements the fieriness of the paste.

Salsa de melocotón Fresh peach salsa

Serves 8

1 garlic clove, finely chopped

3 medium-hot fresh red chillies, deseeded
  and finely chopped

3 spring onions, finely sliced

½ red onion, finely diced

3 fresh ripe peaches or nectarines

juice of 3 limes

½ teaspoon pimentón

pinch of sea salt

freshly ground black pepper

This is a juicy salsa, spiked by the chillies and spices, and it works well as an accompaniment to grilled meat or barbecued chicken. In Mexico, from where it originates, it is most usually served with goat; however, it works equally well with lamb, chicken, or pork. You could use a crisp apple such as a Pink Lady or Braeburn in place of the peaches or nectarines. Or perhaps even make it as a tomato salsa instead.

1 Put the garlic, chilli, spring onion, and red onion in a bowl. Slice the peaches in half but do not peel. Remove the stones and cut the flesh into 1cm (½in) dice. Add to the bowl. Pour over the lime juice (this helps to prevent the peach from discolouring, as well as adding zing).

2 Add the pimentón and sea salt to the salsa, and season with black pepper. Gently stir through until well mixed. Serve as an accompaniment to grilled meat or chicken.

Lezumes en escabeche
Spicy vegetable pickle

This brilliant pickled sauce from Mexico is usually served with tamales, tacos, and empanadas. It is best to make a large amount because it will keep for many weeks.

Makes 1 large glass jar

4 tablespoons rice wine vinegar

4 tablespoons red wine vinegar

3 teaspoons caster sugar

2 teaspoons sea salt

3 allspice berries

2 bay leaves

6 onions, finely chopped, rinsed in cold
  water, and drained

2 carrots, finely chopped

1 red pepper, finely chopped

4 fresh red chillies, deseeded and
  finely chopped

fresh coriander, mint, or flat-leaf
  parsley, finely chopped

1 Bring the rice wine vinegar, red wine vinegar, sugar, salt, allspice, and bay leaves to a simmer in a covered heavy saucepan over a medium-high heat, then remove the pan from the heat.

2 Put the onion, carrot, red pepper, and chilli in a large sterilized glass jar or container with a secure-fitting lid, and pour the vinegar mixture over the top. Allow at least 4 hours for the mixture to cool before using. (The pickle will keep for a long time, but must be refrigerated once opened.)

3 Before using the pickle, put the chopped herbs into a small bowl, then mix with the required amount of vegetable pickle. Serve as an accompaniment to grilled or roasted meat, or the seafood empanadas on pp102–3.

Bistec con chimichurri
Seared steak with chimichurri

Serves 6

6 portion-sized steaks, well hung for
   tenderness and the cut of your choice

a little good-quality olive oil

salt and freshly ground black pepper

For the chimichurri

3 small dried red chillies

3 garlic cloves, peeled

1 teaspoon sea salt

½ teaspoon caster sugar

60ml (2fl oz) vinegar

juice of 2 lemons

100ml (3½fl oz) olive oil

½ bunch of fresh flat-leaf
   parsley, roughly chopped

30 fresh oregano or marjoram
   leaves, roughly chopped

1 To make the chimichurri, crush the dried chillies using a pestle and mortar. Add the garlic, salt, and sugar, and continue pounding until you have a smooth paste. (The salt and sugar will act as abrasives and help to make a purée.) Next add the vinegar and lemon juice to moisten the paste, then mix in the olive oil. Sprinkle in the parsley and oregano, and season with pepper. Taste the sauce and adjust the seasoning if necessary. It should have a bold mix of flavours, to bring out the sweetness of the beef.

2 Heat a little olive oil in a heavy frying pan over a medium heat. When the pan is ready, sear the steak on both sides for a few minutes. Allow the meat to rest for a couple of minutes, and add any juices to the chimichurri. Transfer to serving plates, pour over the chimichurri, and serve immediately. Alternatively, grill the beef instead of searing, or use pork chops or chorizo sausages instead.

Chimichurri is a spectacularly good sauce that is used throughout Argentina, and it is an ever-popular accompaniment to the beef for which that country is famed. It has a very memorable and unique taste which is spicy hot, salty, and sour all at once. I first had it in a market in Buenos Aires, where it was liberally splashed over a grilled chorizo roll. Chimichurri completely transforms any dish of grilled meat or chicken – it's brilliant.

Picarones

Sweet potato and pumpkin doughnuts

These aniseed-infused pumpkin and sweet potato doughnuts are deliciously addictive and very easy to make. Picarones are a popular snack all over Ecuador and Peru, and are traditionally accompanied by "chancaca", a sugarcane syrup. They work very well served piping hot with honey or sugar syrup, or even maple syrup if you prefer. The sweetness of the sweet potato and pumpkin combines beautifully with the spices, black pepper, and salt, topped off with a drizzle of golden honey.

Makes 12–15 doughnuts

250g (9oz) sweet potato, peeled and cut
  into large chunks
250g (9oz) pumpkin or butternut squash,
  peeled and cut into large chunks
1 teaspoon salt
½ teaspoon crushed aniseed

300g (10oz) plain flour
7g (scant ¼oz) dried yeast
oil for frying
freshly ground black pepper
runny honey or sugar syrup or
  maple syrup, to serve

1. Put the sweet potato and pumpkin in a large saucepan with just enough water to soften (don't add too much water, as the sweet potato and pumpkin have enough liquid content of their own – otherwise you will end up with mush). Bring to a boil and simmer until tender, being careful to avoid scorching.

2. Drain off any excess liquid, and mash the sweet potato and pumpkin together to form a smooth purée. Season with the salt, aniseed, and pepper. Transfer to a large bowl, then tip in the flour and combine. Melt the yeast in 4 tablespoons warm water, and mix into the sweet potato mixture to make a fairly firm dough, adding more water or flour if necessary. Cover and leave in a bowl for 2 hours until the dough has doubled in size.

3. Heat the oil for frying. To test if the oil is hot enough, tear off a small ball of dough and shape into a ring by pressing it flat in your hands and making a hole in the centre with your thumb and forefinger. Gently drop the doughnut into the oil, being careful to avoid any spitting from the hot oil, and fry until golden brown on both sides, turning once during the cooking. Drain on kitchen paper. Taste and adjust the seasoning of the dough – it may need a little extra salt or some more aniseed. When you are happy with the seasoning, form the rest of the dough into rings, and fry in batches until pale golden brown on both sides, again turning once during cooking.

4. These are best eaten straight away. Serve piping hot with honey or sugar syrup for drizzling over the top.

Sopa mexicana de flor de calabaza
Mexican pumpkin flower soup

squash flowers such as pumpkin and courgette are found in many recipes across South America. They are delicious, particularly when lightly cooked. In Spain, France, and Italy they crop up in all sorts of recipes. It was fascinating to see them so frequently used around Mexico on all kinds of street stalls and in little cafés, where they would have been appearing in similar recipes for hundreds of years. This fresh summer soup with many of the exciting characteristics of Mexican street food is spiked with a tantalizing edge of green chilli and lime juice.

Serves 6

1 litre (1¾ pints) good-quality chicken stock

a little olive oil

2 fresh green chillies, deseeded and
  finely chopped

2 garlic cloves, finely chopped

1 onion, finely chopped

2 ripe tomatoes

250g (9oz) pumpkin flowers or
  courgette flowers

juice of 2 limes

salt and freshly ground black pepper

1 Bring the chicken stock to the boil in a saucepan. Meanwhile, heat a separate large heavy pan and add a little olive oil. Reserve some of the chilli to garnish the soup, and fry the remainder in the oil with the garlic for about 2 minutes until aromatic. Add the onion and cook until pale golden brown.

2 Cut the tomatoes in half, and grate the open side of each half on a large grater. This is a quick method of getting the pulp from the tomatoes; the skin stays in your hand and can then be discarded. Add the tomato to the pan with the onion. Discard the stems from the pumpkin flowers and roughly chop the flowers, reserving 6 whole flowers to garnish each bowl. When the tomato has cooked down slightly, add the chopped pumpkin flowers to the pan. Cook for 2 minutes until the flowers are wilting. Pour in the hot chicken stock, and season with salt and pepper. Simmer for 5 minutes.

3 While the soup is simmering, heat a small frying pan and add a little olive oil. Fry the reserved whole pumpkin flowers until they are wilted and parts are golden brown. Season with salt and pepper, and add the reserved green chilli. Remove from the heat and set aside to garnish.

4 Using a blender or food processor, purée the soup and return to the pan. Add the lime juice. Taste and adjust the seasoning – there should be a balance between the sweet onion, chicken stock, hot spicy green chilli, and salt. The lime juice wakes up the flavours and provides a delicious sour edge to this simple soup. To serve, pour into bowls and garnish with the whole pumpkin flowers and green chilli.

Empanadas de marisco
Seafood empanadas

Makes 12

olive oil for cooking

2 white onions, finely chopped

2 garlic cloves, finely chopped

2 fresh green chillies, finely chopped

300g (10oz) mussels in their shells

splash of white wine

100g (3½oz) peeled uncooked prawns

200g (7oz) white fish such as hake or cod

3 tomatoes, diced

juice of ½ lemon

½ bunch of coriander, roughly chopped

100g (3½oz) mild Cheddar cheese, grated

sea salt and freshly ground black pepper

For the pastry

175g (6oz) plain flour

125g (4½oz) yellow masa harina

1 teaspoon baking powder

1 teaspoon salt

125g (4½oz) unsalted butter, melted

2 large eggs

1 Heat a little oil in a heavy pan over a medium-high heat. Fry the onion, garlic, and chilli until soft. Remove from the pan. Add the mussels and a splash of white wine to the pan, and cover. Steam for 3 minutes or until the mussels open. Remove the mussels from the pan, discard the shells, and set the meat aside in a bowl. Strain the cooking liquor through a fine sieve and return to a clean pan.

2 Put the prawns, fish, tomato, and onion mixture in the cooking liquor. Simmer gently for about 4 minutes. Season with salt and pepper, and add the lemon juice. Remove the solids with a slotted spoon, and put in the bowl with the mussels. Simmer the cooking liquor until reduced by a third. Pour over the seafood, and add the coriander and grated cheese. Season and set aside.

3 Sift the flour, masa harina, baking powder, and salt into a large bowl. Stir in the cooled melted butter. Whisk 75ml (2½fl oz) water and 1 of the eggs in a small bowl. Add to the flour mixture. Knead for 2 minutes until smooth and pliable.

4 Preheat the oven to 200°C (400°F/Gas 6). Roll out the pastry on a lightly floured surface until 2–3cm (1–1¼in) thick. Cut into 5–6cm (2–2½in) rounds. Place a spoonful of the seafood mixture on the bottom half of each round. Brush the edge of the pastry with egg wash. Fold the top layer of each pastry over to form a half-moon, and crimp the edges together with your thumb and forefinger, squeezing out any air. Bake for 12–15 minutes until golden brown. Serve hot.

Empanadas can be large or small. These are about the size of a Cornish pasty – a substantial snack. The small ones, which are called empanaditas, are great because they consist of about three bites. After which, you can then help yourself to a second or third empanadita! Seafood empanadas are a particular speciality in Ecuador, Argentina, and Chile. Remember, you must be careful with mussels. Before you use them, tap each one lightly on a work surface and discard those that do not close. Once cooked, discard any that remain unopened.

Salsa verde Green tomato salsa

Serves 6

6 unripe green tomatoes

1 onion

2 garlic cloves

4 fresh green chillies, deseeded and
  finely chopped

½ bunch of fresh coriander leaves,
  roughly chopped

2 avocados

½ bunch of fresh parsley, roughly chopped

juice of 2 limes

2 tablespoons olive oil

salt and freshly ground black pepper

In Mexico the two most popular sauces that can accompany just about every dish are salsa roja and salsa verde. There might be only two names for the sauces, but there are hundreds of recipes that vary from stall to stall. Both the red sauce and the green are vibrantly coloured and packed full of flavour, and are great on a filled taco or tortilla. Salsa verde was my favourite of all the sauces that I tasted in Mexico City. You can alter the proportions of the ingredients to suit yourself. If green tomatoes are not available, choose the least-ripe tomatoes that you can find, for sourness.

1 Cut the tomatoes in half. Scoop out the centre core of seeds and place in a sieve over a bowl. Chop the flesh into fine dice and set aside. Cut the onion in half, and grate the flesh so that you are left with a pulp. Set this aside also.

2 Cut the garlic in half and remove any green shoot from the centre (this is part of the garlic that is bitter and can repeat on you). Chop the garlic finely. Using a large pestle and mortar, pound the garlic with the green chilli and a pinch of salt to make a smooth paste. Add half of the coriander leaves and all of the onion to the paste. Still using the pestle and mortar, continue to pound until you have a rough green paste.

3 Using a wooden spoon, push the tomato cores and their seeds through the sieve into the pestle and mortar, extracting all the juice. Discard the seeds and tip any juice that has collected in the bowl into the paste.

4 Halve, peel, and stone the avocado. Cut the flesh into fine 1cm (½in) dice. Add the avocado and green tomato to the paste. Pound a couple of times so part of it is crushed and the remaining part remains as dice. Add the parsley and remaining coriander. Stir through. Next add the lime juice and olive oil, and mix together. Season well with salt and pepper. Check the seasoning. The avocado makes it sweet, the lime juice and green tomato add the sour element, and the green chilli and black pepper supply heat. The salsa should have a real tang and zip to it. Adjust the green chilli content to suit your taste if necessary.

5 Serve in a bowl or on a sandwich, or spread on steak, grilled lamb, grilled chorizo, or sausages. It is great with just about anything.

Mole pipian Pipian sauce with cinnamon

Moles are an integral complex part of Mexican culinary heritage. Areas such as Puebla are famous for them. They date back many centuries, and there are many different types. Some blend chocolate with chilli, which dates back to Aztec times. There are often scores of ingredients blended to a smooth paste. I tasted one version that was a combination of nuts and seeds, and different types of chilli.

Serves 8

3 tablespoons olive oil

2 dried red chillies

1 onion, finely chopped

2 garlic cloves, finely chopped

100g (3½oz) skinless raw peanuts

100g (3½oz) pumpkin seeds

3 cloves

½ teaspoon allspice

½ teaspoon ground cinnamon

½ teaspoon dried thyme

1 chipotle (smoked jalapeño chilli)

1 teaspoon caster sugar

750ml (1¼ pints) chicken stock

juice of 1 lime

sea salt and freshly ground black pepper

1 Heat the olive oil in a pan. Add the dried chillies and fry for a minute to toast them. Transfer the chillies to a bowl, cover with hot water, and soak for 20 minutes. In the same pan, sauté the onion and the garlic, adding a little extra oil if needed.

2 In a separate pan over a gentle heat, first toast the peanuts, then the pumpkin seeds, watching carefully to make sure that they don't burn. Put the peanuts and pumpkin seeds in a food processor, and add the onion/garlic mixture, soaked chillies, cloves, allspice, cinnamon, and thyme. Process with 100ml (3½fl oz) of the chicken stock until smooth, puréeing in small batches if necessary.

3 Return the purée to the pan in which the onion was cooked and gradually heat. Add the remaining chicken stock, and stir until the sauce is the texture of melted ice cream. Taste the sauce. There is a sweetness from the onion and the chicken stock, and the chilli and spices are hot. The roasted nuts and salt provide the savoury qualities. Adjust the seasoning if necessary.

4 Add the lime juice right at the end to wake up the flavours and bring them into balance. Serve with grilled or roasted meat.

Molho de cajú Green cashew nut sauce

Serves 8 or more

4 tablespoons raw cashew nuts

2 garlic cloves

2 fresh green chillies, deseeded and diced

2 shallots, finely diced

100ml (3½fl oz) olive oil or untoasted
    sesame oil

1 tablespoon white wine vinegar

juice of 2 limes

½ bunch of fresh coriander,
    roughly chopped

½ bunch of fresh basil, roughly chopped

pinch of sea salt

freshly ground black pepper

pinch of sugar or a little freshly squeezed
    orange juice (optional)

1   Dry-roast the cashew nuts over a medium heat, watching them carefully and turning them so that they are golden brown all over and do not scorch.

2   To make the sauce, first make a coarse paste of the garlic and chilli in a food processor or blender, then add the shallot and purée to a paste. Now add the cooled cashew nuts, and purée once again until smooth. With the motor running, very gradually add the oil in a thin, steady stream, then add the vinegar and 1 tablespoon water. With the motor on a low speed, add the lime juice, then the coriander and basil, until you have a smooth green paste. Taste and adjust the seasoning with a pinch of sea salt and black pepper, and more lime juice if needed. If the chillies are too hot, add a pinch of caster sugar or some orange juice if you like.

This is a lovely creamy marinade for chicken, beef, or prawns — or anything else that you may be cooking on the grill. Alternatively, the sauce can be used to coat the meat once it is cooked (and still hot). It also makes a tasty dipping sauce and can be served in a small bowl as an accompaniment to a summer barbecue, perhaps with crudités or some fresh crusty bread.

Pudim de abóbora Pumpkin pudding

Serves 4–6

675g (1½lb) pumpkin (choose a sweet
   firm-fleshed variety) or butternut squash,
   cut into cubes

4 large eggs

125g (4½oz) soft brown sugar

½ teaspoon ground cloves

½ teaspoon ground nutmeg

½ teaspoon ground cinnamon

½ teaspoon ground ginger

½ teaspoon salt

250ml (8fl oz) single cream

butter to grease the mould

1. Preheat the oven to 180°C (350°F/Gas 4). Put the pumpkin in a large saucepan with a little water, and cook over a medium heat until soft. Drain, then mash until smooth, removing any stringy bits.

2. Beat the eggs with half the brown sugar until pale and mousse-like. Add the remaining sugar, the spices, and the salt. Mix the cream into the pumpkin purée, then fold in the egg mixture.

3. Lightly butter 6 individual ramekins or moulds. Alternatively, to make one large pudding, butter a 1-litre (1¾-pint) soufflé dish or pudding basin. Set the ramekins (or large dish) in a baking tray and carefully fill the tray with hot water about halfway up the sides of the ramekins (or large dish). Carefully slide into the oven, and bake until set or a toothpick comes out clean – about 40 minutes for individual ramekins; 1 hour 20 minutes for large single pudding. Serve warm with biscotti or similar biscuits.

Sweet pumpkin desserts are very common across South America, and they vary enormously. This recipe came from a small stall in Rio. It has a light creamy texture like a crème brûlée. The delicious combination of brown sugar and the selection of spices makes it very interesting. It should be eaten with little nut biscuits or cookies, and accompanied by an espresso or iced coffee to complete the picture. The Brazilian stall holder was only too pleased to help me with this recipe, offering me more hot pudding and coffee at the same time. It could also be quite easily made into a tart with a pastry base.

Southern Europe

The enjoyment of good food is an integral part
of life across Southern Europe. By extension,
street food is regarded as more than a way
to fuel the body. It is a celebration of strong
traditions, with some recipes being handed
down over centuries and providing a culinary
identity for these countries, as beloved as the
bacon sandwich in Britain or the hamburger
in the United States. Religion and the festivals
that accompany it play a strong role in these
cuisines, with some dishes appearing only
on particular feasts, saints' days, or religious
holidays. There are samplings from Southern
Italy, Sicily, Malta, and Spain. The recipes are
varied, unusual, and not your average fare –
a delicious demonstration of these cuisines.

Day 46: Catania, Sicily On the first day of my stay in Catania, I was walking through a rundown area of the city on a cold, crisp day in February. The majority of the small rough-looking businesses were either motorcycle repair shops or butchers specializing in horsemeat. From a distance, I spied a jewel of a stall on the street corner. Plumes of blue smoke could be seen as I walked down the hill towards it, following the scent like a hound. It was not until I was right there that I saw about 50 small purple artichokes had been grilled in the charcoal, and nestled among the hot coals. They shone out as something delicious on this otherwise dilapidated industrial street. I paid for a couple and got change for a euro. They were anointed with some thick green olive oil, and I was handed a couple of napkins from the pocket of the stall holder. He took another drag of his cigarette and resumed chatting with his two friends while turning some red peppers. I stood by the stall and started to peel the most burnt leaves from the outside, dropping them into a cardboard box on the pavement. The inside was delicious and filled with vibrant green stuffing. Oil oozed out and ran down my wrist, but I didn't really care, as I stood by the charcoal fire eating some of the most delicious morsels that I can remember.

Day 48: Catania, Sicily I was walking towards the train station on my way to Palermo, the island's main city. My bags were heavy and it was cold, but I had heard that there were good examples of street food and typical regional snacks around this bit of town. Pretty soon I found such a place, and the food inside was definitely worth the hardship. The dingy interior was taken up by a large open-fronted wood oven. Across the oven were four or so long metal spits with small baby chickens roasting in front of the fire. Beneath the chickens on the floor of the oven was a large tray of hand-cut chips, catching all the dripping juices from the chickens being idly turned by the barrel-chested owner. Family members were leaning over the wooden counter, watching a loud Italian quiz show on a mounted television in the corner of the room – a familiar sight found in fast-food restaurants, cafés, and takeaway shops the world over. The big difference was that the food being served was exceptionally fresh and tasty. I was hardly able to wait patiently. I ordered my half a chicken, and it was wrapped in foil with some chips. I eagerly took it outside, found a sunlit square, and sat on a stone bench to enjoy the crisp, juicy roast chicken with its generous onion, olive, rosemary, and chilli stuffing (see pp120–1).

Crispeddi Semolina flour fritters

Serves 6–8

25g (scant 1oz) fresh yeast	1 teaspoon chopped fresh finocchio
300ml (10fl oz) hot water	(sweet fennel) fronds or ½ teaspoon
600–700g (1lb 5oz–1lb 9oz) semolina flour	crushed fennel seeds
180g (6oz) fresh ricotta	pinch of sea salt
4 salted anchovies, chopped	pinch of caster sugar
1 tablespoon salted capers, rinsed, drained,	light olive oil for frying
squeezed dry, and chopped	freshly ground black pepper

1 Mix the yeast with a little of the hot water to make a paste. Put the semolina flour in a large bowl. Make a well in the centre, add the yeast paste and remaining hot water, and whisk to make a batter. Leave to rise for 2 hours, as you would with bread dough.

2 Mix the ricotta with the anchovy and capers. Add lots of black pepper and the fennel, salt, and sugar. Roll the ricotta mixture into balls about 2cm (¾in) in diameter. Use a little oil on your hands so that they do not stick. Heat the oil in a heavy pan over a medium-high heat. Dip the balls into the batter and, using a spoon, drop very gently into the pan to avoid splashing. Fry for 4–5 minutes until golden brown on all sides. Drain on kitchen paper and serve immediately.

Panelle (chickpea fritters) This much-loved Sicilian street snack is often served sandwiched in a ciabatta roll. It is best eaten piping hot and fresh from the oven. Mix 500g (1lb 2oz) chickpea flour with a pinch of salt, 2 tablespoons olive oil and 1.5 litres (2¾ pints) water in a heavy saucepan. Cook over a medium heat, stirring continuously with a wooden spoon, to avoid the mixture sticking. Continue cooking for 20 minutes, or until the mixture starts to pull away from the edges. Season with salt and black pepper. Line a bread tin with cling film. Pour the batter into the tin, and cover the surface with another layer of cling film. Leave to set for at least 2 hours. Heat a baking tray in the oven at 200°C (400°F/gas 6). Turn out the *panelle* loaf and cut into thin slices. Remove the tray from the oven and add a splash of olive oil. Place the slices on the tray and return to the oven. Check after 4 minutes and, when the slices are golden brown, turn over to brown on the other side. Serve at once with freshly grated Parmesan, roughly chopped fresh flat-leaf parsley, some lemon wedges, and grindings of black pepper.

These snacks are eaten on market days or the saint's day of a town or village. They are perfect to be shared among friends and are great with drinks to start an evening. Sunblush, or semi-dried, tomatoes marinated in oregano and olive oil can be added to the ricotta mixture with or without the anchovies. Or try pieces of cooked bacon or roughly chopped pitted olives instead. You can even omit the anchovies and simply use fresh herbs such as basil and parsley, or rocket.

Cipolle d'inverno e pancetta alla griglia Grilled spring onions wrapped in pancetta

I had this deliciously simple and very tasty snack late at night when I was in Palermo in Sicily, where it was being grilled in a square near some late-night drinking haunts. Despite the freezing February weather, everyone was drinking and eating outside, with many people huddled around large barbecue grills where lots of tasty things were being cooked. The air was thick with the smoke and aromas of cooking food, and there were hungry partygoers hopping from foot to foot expectantly, waiting for their bread rolls to be removed from the grill.

Serves 8

24 spring onions, trimmed and peeled
good-quality olive oil
16 thin pancetta slices
2 lemons, cut into wedges
crushed dried chilli flakes

a few fresh basil or rocket leaves (optional)
fresh Italian bread such as ciabatta, panini, or focaccia, or other crusty bread rolls
salt and freshly ground black pepper

1 Place the spring onions in a bowl, and pour over a little olive oil. Season well with salt and pepper, and mix together so that the spring onions are coated with the oil and the seasoning.

2 On a clean work surface, lay out two strips of pancetta side by side, with the long sides together. Repeat with all the pancetta, so that you have a bit of a production line. Place 3 spring onions at one end of each of the pancetta strips, and roll the pancetta tightly around the spring onions so that they are covered. Grill on a preheated hot barbecue or griddle pan, or under a hot grill, for a couple of minutes on each side until golden and crispy. Transfer to a chopping board, and cut into small 2cm (¾in) chunks with a large sharp knife. (Cutting up the spring onions makes them much easier to eat.)

3 Split open a crusty bread roll and put the pieces inside. Drizzle with a little olive oil. Season with salt and pepper. Squeeze a little lemon juice over the top, and sprinkle with a little crushed dried chilli flakes. Add a few basil or rocket leaves (if using). Sandwich the filled roll together, and place on the barbecue or under the grill for a couple of minutes each side so that it is toasted.

4 Eat immediately, with your sleeves rolled up and lots of paper napkins on hand. This dish is ideal as part of a summer picnic or barbecue, or as a starter before the main pieces of meat or fish are grilled. Alternatively, chop the grilled spring onion into pieces, pile on top of crostini, drizzle with a little olive oil, and sprinkle with chopped basil or rocket. Season with the lemon and chilli, and eat with your fingers with drinks.

Pastizzi tar-rikotta
Savoury ricotta-filled pastries

Makes 15–20

For the pastry

400g (14oz) plain flour, sifted

½ teaspoon salt

125–150g (4½–5½oz) lard or butter

For the filling

400g (14oz) ricotta

3 eggs, beaten

salt and freshly ground black pepper

1 To make the pastry, mix the flour and salt with about 200ml (7fl oz) cold water in a bowl until it forms a soft, pliable but not sticky dough. Knead well, then leave to rest for about 1½ hours. Set the dough on a floured work surface and cut into 3 pieces. Roll each piece into a long rectangle about 4cm (1¾in) wide. Roll, stretch, and pull each one into long strips. Spread half the lard over the entire length of each strip of dough, first with a palette knife, then with clean, dry hands. Take one end of one strip of the dough and roll it up like a Swiss roll (when rolling it up, do it unevenly – sometimes turning the dough tightly; sometimes more loosely). Repeat with the remaining two strips of dough. Rest the dough in the refrigerator for at least 30 minutes.

2 Take the rolled strips of dough out of the refrigerator and roll them flat again on a floured work surface. Spread with the remaining lard. Roll the strips like a Swiss roll once again, this time in a different direction from the first roll – all this rolling enhances the flakiness of the finished pastry. Rest the pastry in the refrigerator for another 30 minutes.

3 Preheat the oven to 200°C (400°F/Gas 6). To make the filling, put the ricotta in a bowl and season with salt and pepper. Mash the ricotta with a fork, then add the beaten egg. Using a sharp knife, cut off pieces of dough 2–3cm (¾–1¼in) in diameter (about the size of a squash ball). Next, using your fingers and thumb, press out each ball so that it is a thin flat disc. Put a tablespoon of the seasoned ricotta cheese mix in the middle of each circle. Fold each circle from the top and the bottom to the centre, and squeeze the edges of the pastry together with your fingers so that the pocket is sealed (the horizontal ends are formed into points). Place the pastizzi on a lightly oiled baking sheet, and bake in the oven for 20 minutes until the pastry is golden and flaky.

In Malta pastizzi are traditionally eaten for breakfast. They are a delicious and hearty way to start the day if you are setting off early. In fact they are great at any time when eaten fresh from the oven. The most popular and cheapest Maltese street food, pastizzi can be bought from small shops and stalls called "pastizzeriji" which are spread around the island. The two main types are pastizzi "tar-rikotta" (cheese) and pastizzi "tal-pizelli" (peas). These rich diamond-shaped flaky pastries are best eaten hot, with lots of napkins.

spit-roasted chicken and chips in foil eaten on a park bench in winter is one of my great memories from my trips to sicily. I bought this fabulous takeaway dish from one of the many family-run eateries dotted around Catania. The hand-cut chips cooked in the juices dripping from the chickens added another layer of moreishness to the repast. There are lots of different flavours here, and the combination stimulates all the taste buds. It is very easy to bulk up the stuffing to make this dish for more people.

Pollo con olive, cipolla e rosmarino ripieno Poussin stuffed with olives, onion, and rosemary

Serves 4

4 onions, finely sliced

100g (3½oz) black olives, pitted and roughly chopped

5 fresh rosemary sprigs, chopped

4 garlic cloves, halved and any green inner shoot discarded

2 small dried red chillies, crushed

2 tablespoons olive oil plus a little extra

juice of 1 lemon

4 poussins or baby chickens, about 500g (1lb 2oz) each

salt and freshly ground black pepper

1 Preheat the oven 200°C (400°F/Gas 6). Put the onion in a bowl. Mix the olives and rosemary together, and add to the onion. Finely chop the garlic with the dried chilli. Add to the onion mixture with the 2 tablespoons olive oil and the lemon juice. Mix well and season with salt and pepper. Stuff each chicken with a generous amount of the stuffing.

2 Heat a little oil in a heavy ovenproof pan over a medium-high heat. Season the outside of the chickens with salt and pepper. Brown the chickens in the pan on both breasts and the back. When browned, transfer the whole pan to the oven and roast for 30–35 minutes until the meat is tender, basting regularly with all the roasting juices. (If cooking a larger chicken, allow a longer cooking time – usually 1 hour to 1 hour 20 minutes or so.) To check, insert the point of a small knife by the bone; if the juices run clear, the chicken is cooked.

3 Serve the small roasted chickens with piping-hot home-made chips or roast potatoes, or with a fresh salad with bitter and peppery leaves.

Note To try to be more authentic (but without using a spit or rotisserie), place a tray of hand-cut chips splashed with a little olive oil and seasoned with salt and pepper at the bottom of the oven while you are cooking the chicken. Put the chicken on a rack above the chips, so that all the juices drip onto the potatoes. Turn the potatoes regularly during cooking, and pour any leftover juices from inside the chicken over the top just before serving.

Ravioli di Carnalivari Sweet fried ravioli

Serves 6

For the pasta

500g (1lb 2oz) Italian tipo 00 flour

85g (3oz) caster sugar

pinch of sea salt

85g (3oz) unsalted butter

1 egg yolk

1 teaspoon vanilla essence

50ml (2fl oz) milk

grated zest of 1 lemon

½ teaspoon ground cinnamon

1 teaspoon vanilla essence

45g (1½oz) dark chocolate (at least
  70% cocoa solids), grated

2 tablespoons candied orange and
  lemon peel, finely chopped

For the filling

350g (12oz) fresh ricotta cheese

100g (3½oz) caster sugar

a little beaten egg yolk for brushing

about 300ml (10fl oz) light olive oil

icing sugar for dusting

These are really delicious, and the creamy filling is a treasure trove of unexpected flavours. I love things such as this where you have no idea of what is awaiting inside until you take your first bite. Similar pastries to these are made in Sicily, Sardinia, Malta, and across the Mediterranean.

1 To make the pasta, rub the flour, sugar, salt, and butter together until the texture of breadcrumbs. Mix in the egg yolk, vanilla essence, and milk to form a small ball of dough. Leave to rest for 30 minutes.

2 Meanwhile, mix together the ricotta, caster sugar, lemon zest, cinnamon, and vanilla until smooth. Stir in the chocolate and orange and lemon peel. Taste and adjust the flavours to your liking.

3 To finish the ravioli, roll out the pastry until ½cm (¼in) thick. Using a biscuit cutter or small plate, cut into discs 10–12cm (4–5in) in diameter. Spoon the ricotta paste onto the bottom half of the disc, in a half-moon shape, leaving a small rim. Brush the rim with egg yolk. Fold the pastry over and, with a cupped hand, carefully squeeze any air bubbles out of the filling. Seal the edges tightly – otherwise the ravioli will open and explode when cooking.

4 Heat the olive oil over a medium-high heat. When hot, shallow-fry 2 or 3 pastries at a time in batches. Cook for 3–4 minutes until golden all over. Drain on kitchen paper. Leave to cool, then dust with icing sugar and serve.

Variation For a different taste, swap the candied peel for dried fruits such as figs and apricots. Or you could swap them for roasted pistachio nuts, or perhaps a coffee and chocolate combination.

Triglie de scoglio

Pan-fried red mullet with preserved lemon, olives, and parsley

The key to cooking a delicate fish such as red mullet is its absolute freshness. I had this dish at a small outdoor café near Catania's fish market. There were only a few dishes on the menu, and most of the customers of the surrounding cafés were market traders and other local characters all enjoying red mullet, crusty bread, and local white wine. The proprietor was cooking the mullet in large fish-shaped black pans, with about 8 small fish in each one. This is an impressive dish, but is not complicated to make. The stuffing can also be used for chicken breasts.

Serves 4

2 lemons

3 tablespoons rock salt

1 garlic clove, halved and any green inner shoot discarded

30 black olives, pitted and roughly chopped

½–1 fresh red chilli, seeded and finely chopped

20 fresh basil leaves, roughly chopped

20 fresh flat-leaf parsley leaves, roughly chopped

juice of 1 lemon

2 tablespoons extra virgin olive oil

4 fresh red mullet, 250–400g (9–14oz) each, gutted, scaled, and cleaned

a little light olive oil

sea salt and freshly ground black pepper

1 To make the preserved lemon, put the lemons into a small, tight-fitting pan. Cover with water and add the rock salt. Place a small lid or saucer on top of the lemons to keep them submerged. Bring to a boil, and simmer until soft to the point of a knife (8–10 minutes). Refresh under cold water. When the lemons are cool, cut in half, remove all the flesh and pith, and discard. Using a thin sharp knife, trim the inside of the skin, removing any remaining traces of the bitter pith. You are left with lozenge-shaped pieces of lemon skin. Finely chop and set aside.

2 Preheat the oven to 180°C (350°F/Gas 4). Crush the garlic with a little sea salt using the back of a knife, until you have a smooth paste. Mix the garlic, olives, chilli, basil, parsley, and preserved lemon together in a bowl. Add the lemon juice and olive oil, and season with salt and pepper.

3 Take one of the red mullet and pat dry with kitchen paper. Stuff the cavity with a portion of the olive and lemon mixture. Repeat the process with the remaining mullet. Season the fish inside and out with salt and pepper. Heat a little oil in an frying pan over a medium-high heat. Pan-fry the mullet for 3 minutes. Very gently turn over and cook on the other side for 2 minutes. Transfer the mullet to a baking dish and slide into the oven. Bake for 5 minutes until cooked. (You could also barbecue or grill the fish, or bake entirely in a conventional oven.) Serve immediately with some mixed leaves or braised spinach. The smoky roasted mullet combines brilliantly with the stuffing.

Mustazzoli Honey and nut pastries

Serves 4–6

For the pastry

400g (14oz) plain white flour

100g (3½oz) lard or unsalted butter

150g (5½oz) caster sugar

2 eggs

2–4 tablespoons milk

For the filling

350g (12oz) mixture of fresh walnuts,
   almonds, and pine nuts

140g (5oz) honey

2 tablespoons plain white flour

grated zest of 1 orange

1 teaspoon almond essence

icing sugar for dusting

1 To make the pastry, sift the flour into a bowl. Rub 85g (3oz) of the lard into the flour between your fingers, until it resembles the texture of breadcrumbs. Mix in the sugar, then add the eggs and milk, until you have a soft pastry. Cover and refrigerate for at least 1 hour. Make the filling while the pastry is resting.

2 Heat the oven to 180°C (350°F/Gas 4). Place the nuts on a baking sheet, and roast for 2–3 minutes until golden brown all over, shaking halfway through to make sure they do not scorch. Remove the nuts from the oven, and increase the oven temperature to 200°C (400°F/Gas 6).

3 Add the honey to a small pan, and dilute it with 4 tablespoons water. Bring the liquid to the boil. Stir in the flour, little by little, until you have a smooth paste. Add the orange zest and almond essence. Roughly chop the roasted nuts and stir them in. Remove from the heat, and leave to cool completely.

4 To make the pastries, divide the dough into two pieces. Roll out the first half of the pastry to form a rectangle approximately 5 x 10cm (2 x 4in) and ½cm (¼in) thick. Spoon half the nut mixture onto the long side of the pastry rectangles, and roll the pastry over a couple of times to make a long nut swirl. Repeat with the second half of the pastry. Use the remaining lard to grease a length of baking parchment as long as the pastry rolls. Place the baking parchment on a baking sheet, then place the rolls onto the baking parchment. Cut the rolls into small squares of roughly 2cm (¾in) – the shapes can be a little irregular. Bake in the oven for 15–20 minutes until golden. Remove from the oven and allow to cool. Dust the finished pastries with icing sugar and serve.

These nut pastries make a great snack with a cup of strong coffee, mint tea, or alongside a bowl of vanilla ice cream. Variations of this sort of pastry can be found around the Mediterranean in any place where nuts are grown, from the islands of Sicily, Sardinia, and Malta, to Turkey, Lebanon, and Morocco.

Carciofi ripieni alla griglia

Grilled artichokes with garlic, chilli, and pine nuts

These artichokes are perfect for a summer picnic or starter for a barbecue. In Catania where I had them, they were eaten on the street as a hearty snack. I was there in February and it was very cold. It probably seemed a lot colder because I didn't have enough of the right clothes to wear as my luggage had been lost, but these sweet, smoky morsels somehow made all my troubles recede. There is no polite way to eat these – simply roll up your sleeves and dig in. When you get to the heart, you can pretty much eat it in one or two mouthfuls.

Serves 4–6

100g (3 oz) pine nuts

4 garlic cloves, halved and any green inner shoot removed

2 small dried red chillies

1 small bunch of fresh flat-leaf parsley, leaves picked and finely chopped

3 tablespoons good-quality extra virgin olive oil plus extra for serving

juice of 2 lemons

18 small violet-tinged artichokes (in season in spring and early summer)

salt and freshly ground black pepper

lemon wedges to serve

1 Heat a charcoal barbecue until the coals are white-hot. Toast the pine nuts in a dry frying pan over a medium-high heat for 2–3 minutes until golden brown. Watch carefully as they scorch very easily. Finely chop the garlic, and finely crush the dried chilli with a pinch of salt. Mix the pine nuts, garlic, chilli, and parsley with the olive oil and lemon juice. Season well with salt and pepper.

2 Take an artichoke and trim down the stem. Prise the leaves apart, without pulling them off. Work your way to the centre of the artichoke. Using a teaspoon, remove the hairy choke by scraping in a circular motion. Take a teaspoon of pine nut mixture and push it down towards the base. Add another spoonful of filling and spread it among the central inner leaves. Repeat with the remaining artichokes. Season the inside of the artichokes with salt and pepper.

3 Carefully place the artichokes among the white-hot coals, keeping them vertical. Grill for 8–10 minutes, turning occasionally and cooking in batches if necessary. To test whether they are cooked, hold one with a pair of tongs. Insert the point of small sharp knife into the base just above the stem. It should be soft. If not, cook for a few more minutes. Remove from the heat. Cool slightly.

4 Have some extra virgin olive oil and the lemon wedges ready. Pull off the blackened outside leaves and discard. Pour a little extra virgin olive oil into the centre and squeeze over some lemon juice. Peel off and eat the inner leaves. The soft, pale centre can be eaten in a couple of mouthfuls, stalks and all.

Croquetas de bacalao Salt cod croquettes

Bacalao, or salt cod, is very popular across the Mediterranean, in Portugal, Spain, and Italy, where it can be found in a number of dishes. I sampled this particular version, delicious fresh-cooked croquettes, at a stall in a market in southern Spain. Drawn by the lovely aroma, I tracked my way around the stalls until I found the person who was responsible for these tasty snacks.

Serves 4–6

200g (7oz) salt cod, soaked in several
changes of cold water in the refrigerator
for 24 hours (or use skinless, boneless
cod fillet)

500ml (16fl oz) milk

2 bay leaves

300g (10oz) floury potatoes, peeled and
cut into large chunks

1 shallot, peeled and finely grated

1 tablespoon plain flour

1 bunch of fresh flat-leaf parsley,
roughly chopped

½ teaspoon pimentón

sunflower oil for frying

salt and freshly ground black pepper

1 Drain the salt cod and rinse well. Place in a saucepan with the milk and bay leaves. Slowly bring to the boil, and simmer gently for 4–5 minutes. Using a slotted spoon, transfer the cod from the pan to a large bowl, then put the potatoes into the same pan. Top up with water to cover if necessary, and simmer for 15–20 minutes.

2 Meanwhile, shred the cooked salt cod with your fingers, and mix with the shallot, flour, three-quarters of the parsley, and pimentón in a bowl. Drain the potatoes well, and add to the cod mixture. Use a potato masher to mash everything together; it can be quite coarsely mashed. Taste and season with salt and pepper if necessary. The mixture should be salty and sweet, with a warmth from the pimentón and black pepper. Scoop out spoonfuls of the mixture, form roughly into oval shapes of a size that can be eaten in one or two mouthfuls, and space the croquettes out on a floured tray.

3 Heat sunflower oil to a depth of about 3cm (1½in) in a large heavy saucepan over a medium-high heat for 5 minutes until shimmering, or until a small amount of the croquette mixture turns golden in about 45 seconds. Carefully lower 6 croquettes into the oil, one by one, using a slotted spoon. As soon as they turn golden on all sides (3–4 minutes), remove with the slotted spoon and drain on kitchen paper, keeping them warm while you fry the remaining croquettes in the same way. Serve up straight away with generous spoonfuls of a tomato dipping sauce or salsa.

Quaglie marinate con salsa di capperi
Marinated quail with caper sauce

Sicilian food is fascinating because it often combines sweet flavours with sour, salty, and peppery hot elements. Honey and vinegar are commonly used in Sicilian dressings and marinades. I had this at a small country fair in Sicily. You could smell something good long before you got to the queue by the large barbecue pit. A simple dish to make at home, even if there are a few different stages, it works well served on a bed of herbed couscous, bulgur wheat salad, or a pilaf of rice or pearl barley. Try it with partridge or baby chickens, or even as skewers of chicken breast.

Serves 4 as a starter

2 quails

2 garlic cloves, finely chopped

1 small dried red chilli, finely crushed

pinch of salt

finely grated zest and juice of 1 lemon

1 tablespoon finely chopped fresh
   marjoram, thyme, or oregano leaves

1 tablespoon red wine vinegar

1 tablespoon runny honey

1 glass white wine

2 tablespoons roughly chopped fresh
   flat-leaf parsley

2 tablespoons pine nuts or blanched
   almonds, dry-roasted until pale golden

freshly ground black pepper

For the caper sauce

1 preserved lemon (see p124), chopped

1 tablespoon salted capers, rinsed, drained,
   squeezed dry, and chopped

2 tablespoons roughly chopped fresh
   marjoram or basil leaves

1 tablespoon red wine vinegar

3 tablespoons extra virgin olive oil

1 Soak 4 bamboo skewers in cold water for at least 30 minutes. Turn the first quail onto its front. Using a pair of kitchen scissors, carefully cut around the triangular piece of the backbone and remove with the wishbone attached. Use the side of a heavy-backed knife to flatten the bird. Insert a bamboo skewer through a wing, then through the leg meat. Repeat on the other side so that the bird is pinned flat. Repeat this process with the other quail.

2 Work the garlic and chilli on a board with a pinch of salt to make a paste. Combine with the remaining marinade ingredients (not the parsley and pine nuts) in a shallow glass or ceramic dish. Add the quails and season with pepper. Marinate in the refrigerator for at least 2 hours. Combine all the ingredients for the caper sauce. Check the seasoning – it should be salty and sour.

3 Preheat the oven to 220°C (425°F/Gas 7). Heat an ovenproof griddle pan until very hot. Remove the birds from the marinade and season. Grill skin-side down for 3–4 minutes until a deep, rich brown. Turn over and transfer the whole pan to the oven for 5 minutes. (The juices should run rose pink when a knife is inserted close to the leg bone.) Pour the remaining marinade into a small pan and reduce by half (3–4 minutes). Serve with the hot sauce poured over the birds, with a spoonful of caper sauce and a scattering of pine nuts and parsley.

Cudduruni Sicilian focaccia-style bread

Makes 2 large pizzas or 8 smaller ones

For the biga

2.5g (1⁄16oz) fresh yeast

150ml (5fl oz) warm water

125g (4½oz) strong white flour

For the dough

7g (scant ¼oz) fresh yeast

1 teaspoon sugar

350ml (12fl oz) warm water

7 tablespoons biga

3 tablespoons olive oil

450g (1lb) strong plain flour

1½ teaspoons salt

Italy has always been famous for its breads – they have a delicious smell and a wonderful open, aerated texture. This is largely due to what is called "biga", a fresh yeast starter. In traditional bakeries the starter is kept going for decades, handed from one generation to another. Plan ahead and make your starter the day before. Cudduruni is similar to focaccia, and can have various open toppings, or be topped, rolled over, and sealed like a calzone. It is also served more simply as rounds of dough, fried until golden on both sides, and sprinkled with salt.

1 To make the biga, or starter, crumble the yeast into the warm water and add the flour. Mix together until you have a thick batter. Cover with a damp tea cloth, and leave at room temperature to ferment for at least 6 hours or overnight. The biga may separate in this period of time; simply stir it back together. (To keep your biga going, feed with a bit of warm water and flour each day, and mix together, or simply mix in a small offcut from the fresh dough.)

2 To make the dough, mix the yeast and the sugar, and break up with a teaspoon until you have a smooth paste. Whisk this into the warm water with the biga and the olive oil. Sift the flour and salt into a bowl, and mix in the yeast liquid. Mix together until you form a dough. Turn onto a floured board, and knead vigorously for 12–15 minutes until the dough is shiny and elastic. It should be springy to the touch.

3 Lightly flour a bowl and place the ball of dough in it. Cover and leave in a warm place until it has doubled in size, about 1½ hours.

Two types of bread To make a simple loaf, flour a baking tray and shape the dough on the tray. Allow to prove for 10 minutes. Bake in a preheated 220°C (425°F/Gas 7) oven for 25–35 minutes until golden, depending on the size and depth of the loaf. It is ready when the loaf sounds hollow when knocked on the bottom. Alternatively, take pieces of dough about the size of tennis balls and flatten until 1cm (½in) thick. Heat a splash of olive oil in a heavy pan over a medium-high heat. Fry the rounds one at a time, cooking for 2–3 minutes on one side until golden. Turn over and fry for 2 more minutes on the other side. Sprinkle with sea salt and drizzle with some extra virgin olive oil. Eat piping hot.

Calzone con tonne, broccoli e ricotta

Grilled tuna, sprouting broccoli, and ricotta calzone

Makes 6 medium calzone

300g (10oz) fresh tuna, cut into steaks
about 2cm (¾in) thick

200g (7oz) purple sprouting broccoli, cut
into equal-sized florets

4 tablespoons good-quality olive oil

30 fresh basil leaves, roughly chopped

juice of 1 lemon

2 small dried chillies

2 garlic cloves, peeled

200g (7oz) ricotta cheese

1 quantity cudduruni dough (see p134)

salt and freshly ground black pepper

1 Preheat the oven to 200°–220°C (400°–425°F/Gas 6–7). Heat a char-grill
or griddle pan until very hot. Season the tuna well with salt and pepper, and
add the olive oil. Grill for about 2 minutes on each flat side (3–4 minutes in total)
until the flesh is cooked medium rare. Remove from the pan and set aside.

2 Put the broccoli in a bowl and add a little olive oil. Season with salt and
pepper. Mix together. Grill the broccoli on the char-grill or in the griddle pan
for 3 minutes. Break the tuna into smaller pieces, and mix with the grilled broccoli
in a bowl. Add the basil and lemon juice.

3 Crush the dried chilli with the garlic and a little salt to make a smooth
paste. Using a fork, mix the garlic paste into the ricotta. Do not overbeat
the ricotta, as you want it to still have some texture and air in it. Season well with
lots of black pepper.

4 Roll out the dough into a circle ½cm (¼in) thick. Spread the ricotta over
the dough base, leaving a 2cm (¾in) border around the edge. Scatter the
tuna-broccoli mixture over half of the base. Sprinkle with a little extra good olive
oil. Fold the top edge over, and pinch the edges together using your finger and
thumb. Give the dough little twists to keep it all sealed. Brush the outside with a
little oil, and bake in the oven for 10–12 minutes until golden brown and crisp.

This filled pizza, or calzone, came from a busy baker's shop overlooking the market in Catania. Most of the pizza emanating from this establishment never went further than about six feet outside the shopfront. The flavours of this filling were unexpected, yet it was spectacular – hence the 20 or so people standing and eating a slice. You could easily make this as small snack-sized calzone.

Cudduruni con patate, salsiccie e pomodori secchi Potato, spiced sausage, and semi-dried tomato pizza

Makes 6–8 small pizzas or 2 large ones

250g (9oz) new potatoes, scrubbed and thinly sliced

2 garlic cloves

4 tablespoons olive oil

1 quantity cudduruni dough (see p134)

100g (3½oz) spicy Italian dried pork sausage or other pork sausage such as chorizo, cut into slices

60g (2oz) sunblush tomatoes (these semi-dried tomatoes are available from delicatessens and good supermarkets), chopped

4 teaspoons finely chopped fresh rosemary leaves

125g (4½oz) pecorino, grated

sea salt and freshly ground black pepper

1 Preheat the oven to 220°C (425°F/Gas 7). Blanch the potatoes in a pan of boiling water for 5 minutes, then drain in a colander and leave to dry. Crush the garlic with a little salt, then mix with the olive oil.

2 Once it has rested, punch down the centre of the cudduruni dough to knock any air from it. Knead in the bowl for a couple of minutes. You can make this as either small individual pizzas or two larger ones. The large pizzas do not have to be an even shape; you can even make a large square slab if you wish. If making individual pizzas, break the dough into even-sized balls a little smaller than a tennis ball. Roll the dough out on a floured work surface until thin and even – about ½cm (¼in) thick.

3 Brush the rolled piece of dough with the crushed garlic and olive oil mixture, then scatter the potato over the top. Next scatter over the sausage and sunblush tomato. Sprinkle with the rosemary and finally the pecorino. Drizzle with some more of the olive oil and garlic mixture, and season well with pepper and some sea salt. (Remember that the sausage and cheese will be quite salty.)

4 Bake in the oven for 10–12 minutes until the base is golden brown on the bottom. Serve immediately, cut into slices if necessary.

This is one of two versions of pizza I ate in Sicily. It has a very tasty topping of sliced potatoes with rosemary, spiced sausage, sun-dried tomato, and pecorino. It is very versatile in how you can serve it – as a snack, canapé, or starter, or as an informal meal. In the bakeries of Catania, it is served in large sheets to be eaten on the hoof while shopping in the market.

Imqaret Date pastries

These very popular sweet snacks are eaten hot from street stalls around the island of Malta. I first had them at the city gate in Valetta, where the vendor was in a shiny stainless-steel trailer similar to one selling hot dogs. You could see him frying large batches of the imqaret in cauldrons of boiling oil. These pastries stem from ancient recipes tracing back to Malta's Arabic past. The sweet date filling is infused with an aniseed flavour. These are great with coffee or tea, or with ice cream or a cream-based dessert such as crème brûlée or panna cotta.

Makes about 30

For the pastry
500g (1lb 2oz) plain flour
pinch of salt
60g (2oz) caster sugar
60g (2oz) butter, roughly cubed
75ml (2½fl oz) soft red wine (not sweet)
60ml (2fl oz) orange juice

For the filling
400g (14oz) pitted dates
juice and grated zest of 1 orange
juice and grated zest of 1 lemon
150ml (5fl oz) soft red wine (not sweet)
pinch of ground cloves
1 bay leaf
4 star anise

vegetable oil for frying

1 To make the pastry, sieve the plain flour and salt into a large bowl. Add the sugar and butter, and rub into the flour between your fingertips to form the texture of breadcrumbs. Using a spoon, mix in the wine and orange juice to make a smooth dough, adding a little extra flour if necessary. Turn the dough out onto a floured work surface, and knead as you would bread dough until it is soft but not sticky. Rest in the refrigerator for at least 30 minutes until needed.

2 Put all the ingredients for the filling in a heavy pan. Simmer gently over a medium heat for 20 minutes until the dates are soft and the wine has reduced. Discard the star anise and the bay leaf. Transfer the filling to a food processor or blender, and process until smooth. Allow to cool completely.

3 When ready, cut the pastry into 4 pieces. Take one of the pieces and roll it out as thinly as possible on a floured work surface, into a strip about 10cm (4in) wide. Using a pastry brush, moisten the edges of the pastry with a little water, and spoon some of the filling in a line down the centre of the pastry. Fold the pastry over the top of the filling from one side to the other, flatten slightly, and press the edges together. You will end up with a long roll. Cut diagonally across the pastry with a sharp knife, making diamond-shaped pieces that are about 5cm (2in) long. Repeat the process with the remaining pastry and date filling.

4 Heat the oil to a depth of about 2cm (¾in) in a heavy pan over a medium-high heat. Break off a small piece of pastry and add to the oil – it should sizzle slightly, but not brown too fast. When ready, shallow-fry the pastries in small batches for 4–5 minutes until golden brown all over. Serve immediately.

The Middle East and North Africa

The cuisine of the Middle East is as ancient and fluid as the history of its peoples. Long-established spice routes, traders, and nomadic cultures have meant similar dishes are made across a vast distance and several countries. Some food styles have not been restricted by geographical boundaries. Other dishes are particular to small regions or even groups of people, and adhere to long-standing traditions that have been handed down for generations.

Day 68: Istanbul, Turkey Istanbul, the city that straddles the continent of Europe on one side and Asia on the other, is full of contrasts and contradictions. This is apparent in the historical buildings such as the mosque of Sophia, once a spectacular Byzantine church from the third century. The layers of history and the different cultures that are present in Istanbul seem to exist in harmony. The same is true of the food. Some things are simple, such as the grilled mackerel sandwiches with tomato and onion that are available on the central bridge that crosses the Golden Horn. Other dishes are much more elaborate, with an intricate layering of exotic spices from the East. One of Istanbul's most famous examples of street food is the delicious *midye dolmasi*, a dish of plump steamed mussels stuffed with short-grain rice, raisins, pine nuts, and a heady mix of cinnamon, ground allspice, paprika, cayenne pepper, and ground cloves. Served with wedges of lemon, these mussels make a great snack. It is amazing that they can be sold so cheaply when someone has had to open the individual mussels with a knife like an oyster. It was after tasting these that I found the grilled sardines given on pp144–5.

Day 74: Marrakesh, Morocco As the February cold creeps in, dusk falls and the market in Marrakesh springs to life in the twilight. At this late hour it as if seems the entire population of Morocco is packed into the market square, which is stacked with painted stalls selling roasted pumpkin seeds, dried figs, juicy dates, apricots, and prunes. There are snake charmers and soothsayers, poets and musicians, all busking and enthusiastically providing the mystical entertainments that have been performed for centuries. Food stalls groan under towers of pistachio and pine nuts, almonds, and walnuts. People crowd onto benches ready for their plates of hot *harira* (see pp166–7), kebabs, and spicy sausages. The hungry customers enjoy dishes of couscous with grilled lamb and other meats, including liver and brains. All are drinking fresh tamarind juice or mint tea – which is always served scalding hot and syrupy sweet. Large pots of snails are being devoured by the bowlful, and huge clouds of aromatic smoke billow from barbecues, blurring the edges of my vision. Women and men are adorned in the unique robes of their tribes, bodies wrapped in layers against the cold winter night. Jumbled into the ancient mix are crappy stereos blasting shallow pop music, and stalls selling mobile phone ringtones. As the scene bombards my senses, I consider my myriad choices for a hearty supper.

Samak a-sardeen mi'l'aaq
Grilled sardines

Serves 4–6

6 bay leaves, roughly chopped

2 tablespoons salt

4 green cardamom pods

2 garlic cloves

2 small dried red chillies

1 teaspoon ground allspice

2 tablespoons olive oil

12 fresh sardines, scaled and gutted,
    gills removed, and cleaned inside and out
    (you can ask your fishmonger to do this)

1 lemon, cut into quarter lengthways,
    then cut into triangular slices

½ bunch of fresh flat-leaf parsley,
    finely chopped

freshly ground black pepper

1 Preheat a charcoal grill, barbecue, or griddle pan until white-hot. Using a pestle and mortar, grind the bay leaves with the salt until you are left with a bright green powder. (This bay leaf salt is delicious on its own and can be used to season roast potatoes or grilled meats or fish.) Add the cardamom pods and continue to grind until fine. Sift the mixture through a sieve into a bowl, so that you remove any husks or pieces of stalk.

2 Crush the garlic, dried chilli, and allspice, again using a pestle and mortar, and mix with the other spices in a bowl. Add the olive oil.

3 Pat the inside of the sardines dry with kitchen paper, then rub some of the spice marinade over the inside and outside of each fish. Mix the lemon slices with the remaining spice marinade. Season with lots of pepper. Add the parsley and mix together. Stuff the sardines with the lemon and parsley mixture.

4 Grill the sardines for 3–4 minutes on each side or until golden brown and crispy on both sides. With small fish such as this, it is important not to overcook the fish – otherwise it will dry out. As the sardines are small and the grill or pan is hot, the sardines will carry on cooking when you remove them from the heat, while you are plating them.

5 Serve these fantastic little fish hot with wedges of lemon, a selection of salads, and lots of fresh bread. The salt, sourness, and heat of the spice marinade and the lemon slices cut the rich fattiness of the fish.

I had these spicy fresh sardines in a small café overlooking the majestic stretch of water in Istanbul called the Golden Horn. I settled back to enjoy my sardines and the view of Istanbul's skyline, liberally scattered with its magnificent mosques, minarets, and other historical architectural wonders. The dish is a classic example of street food that has a simplicity belying its tastiness, relying as it does on the best and freshest ingredients. It is great for the barbecue. The stuffing can also be used for mackerel, red mullet, sea bass, bream, or snapper.

Fetta Stuffed aubergine with yogurt and pine nuts

Serves 4–6

1kg (2¼lb) aubergines

olive oil for frying

7 pitta breads, broken into small triangles,
  plus extra to serve

100g (3½oz) pine nuts

600g (1lb 5oz) lamb mince

1 teaspoon ground allspice plus a little extra

200ml (7fl oz) tomato juice

1 cinnamon stick

2 bay leaves

2 garlic cloves

300ml (10fl oz) Greek-style yogurt

salt and freshly ground black pepper

Fetta is traditionally eaten for breakfast in Lebanon and Syria, and is a very substantial start to the day. I had this version in a small café in Beirut, for an early breakfast before being taken to other similar streetside cafés and breakfast establishments to sample other dishes commonly eaten at the start of a working day. On that particular day, I ate eight different breakfasts across the city, each one as individually filling as this fetta with its irresistible finishing touch of hot garlic-spiked yogurt.

1 Cut the tops off the aubergines and scoop out half the flesh. Soak the aubergines in salted water while you prepare the other ingredients.

2 Heat a heavy pan over a medium-high heat, and add some olive oil. Fry the triangles of pitta bread in batches for a few minutes until crisp and golden brown. Remove from the oil using a slotted spoon or tongs, and drain on kitchen paper. Using the same pan, fry the pine nuts in the oil until golden brown. Remove and drain on kitchen paper.

3 Add a little oil to a separate pan. Fry the meat with the 1 teaspoon allspice until the meat is tender. Season with salt and pepper, and add half the pine nuts. Remove the aubergines from the salted water, and stuff the scooped-out centres with the meat mixture. Fry the stuffed aubergines in the oil until lightly browned underneath, being careful not to disturb the filling.

4 Heat the tomato juice with the cinnamon stick and bay leaves in a large shallow pan. Season with salt and pepper. When the tomato juice is simmering, add the stuffed aubergines and cook gently until the sauce thickens. Meanwhile, heat an overhead grill until hot.

5 Crush the garlic and add to the yogurt. Cover the bottom of an ovenproof dish with the pieces of fried pitta bread, then layer the stuffed aubergines and pour the yogurt over the top. Sprinkle with a little extra allspice. Place the dish under the preheated overhead grill, and cook for a few minutes so that the yogurt is hot and sizzling in places. Garnish with the remaining roasted pine nuts, and serve hot with lots of extra warm pitta bread.

Kibbeh samak Stuffed fish balls

Serves 4–6

450g (1lb) bulghur wheat

1 onion, finely chopped

700g (1½lb) firm white fish

juice of ½ lemon

vegetable oil for frying

salt and freshly ground black pepper

lemon wedges, to serve

fresh coriander, to garnish

For the filling

1 tablespoon olive oil

1 onion, finely chopped

50g (1¾oz) apricots, finely chopped

25g (scant 1oz) pitted dates, finely chopped

small handful of chopped coriander leaves

1 Tip the bulghur wheat into a bowl, cover with cold water, and leave to soak for 10 minutes. Put the onion into a food processor and work until smooth. Add the fish and lemon juice, and season with salt and pepper.

2 Line a sieve with a clean fine dishcloth or a piece of muslin or cheesecloth, and drain the soaked bulghur. Pick up the ends of the cloth and squeeze tightly to remove any excess liquid. Add the bulghur in batches to the fish purée, processing between each addition to form a workable dough. If it needs to be a bit more malleable, add a little iced water.

3 To make the filling, heat the oil in a heavy pan over a medium-high heat. Sauté the onion for 3–4 minutes until softened. Add the apricot, date, and coriander. Season with salt and pepper. Remove from the heat and allow to cool.

4 With moistened hands, divide the fish mixture into 20 or so pieces, and roll into even-sized balls. Using your index finger, make a hole in each ball and fill it with a little of the fruit stuffing. Re-form the ball around the stuffing, and pat into shape. Heat the oil for frying. Cook the fish balls in batches until they are golden brown on all sides. Drain on kitchen paper.

5 Garnish with fresh coriander, and serve warm with lemon wedges. You can easily vary the filling given here slightly, using some chopped nuts, spices, or chopped fresh chilli, or more chopped herbs to suit your taste. Serve as an appetizer or as part of a larger selection of dishes, or as a snack or canapé.

In the ancient Lebanese coastal ports of Sidon and Tyre, cities that were strategically important before the arrival of the Romans, fried patties or cakes known as "kibbeh" are made from fish and stuffed with dried fruits. Kibbeh are usually made with lamb and are a traditional snack across Lebanon and the Middle East. Varieties range from spicy to mild; with nuts or without. Some use prime minced lamb and are eaten raw; others are fried or baked. Their shape varies from small balls to large egg shapes or flatter pockets like small pitta breads.

Shourba corbasi
Chard soup with rice and turmeric

Serves 4–6

500g (1lb 2oz) chard leaves or spinach
  leaves or beetroot tops (stalks removed)
  or combination of all three
1.2 litres (2 pints) good-quality vegetable
  or chicken stock
2 tablespoons olive oil
2 onions, finely chopped
2 leeks, rinsed, halved lengthways, and
  finely sliced into half-moons

100g (3½oz) long-grain rice
2 tablespoons white wine vinegar
2 garlic cloves, finely chopped
350g (12oz) plain Greek-style yogurt
large pinch of ground turmeric
juice of 1 lemon
½ bunch of fresh mint, leaves picked and
  roughly chopped
salt and freshly ground black pepper

This wholesome springtime soup is commonly served all over the Mediterranean and Middle East. It uses the freshest ingredients and, as the vegetables are not cooked for long, the soup keeps its bright colour, all its flavour, and so its nutrients. Try different combinations of greens – swiss chard and silverbeet also work well. I had this soup at a simple café within a vegetable market where all these vegetables were being sold. In terms of distance, the food travelled a matter of a few feet from market stall to saucepan. Serve in spring and early summer.

1 Finely dice the stalks of the chard leaves. Rinse the leaves and finely shred. Bring the stock to the boil in a saucepan.

2 Heat the oil in a heavy pan or casserole over a medium-high heat. Add the onion, leek, and chard stems, and sweat for 4–5 minutes until slightly coloured. Add the rice and cook for 2 minutes, to coat in the oil and absorb the flavours. Season with salt and pepper. Pour in the hot stock and vinegar, and bring to the boil. Once boiling, reduce the heat and simmer for 12–15 minutes or until the rice is tender. While the soup is simmering, crush the garlic with a little salt. Add to the yogurt with the turmeric and half the lemon juice. Mix together, then taste and season with salt and pepper.

3 When the rice is tender, add the shredded chard leaves to the soup. Continue to simmer for about 3 minutes until the leaves are cooked. Remove from the heat and whisk in the yogurt mixture, then add the mint. Check the seasoning, adding a little extra lemon juice or cracked black pepper if liked. Serve warm or at room temperature, to best appreciate the flavours.

Beetroot tops Beetroot leaves, or tops, make a great extra vegetable, which you often get for free when you buy beetroot. They are delicious when blanched and sautéed, providing a delicious sweetness combined with an irony earthiness. The Italians use beetroot tops a lot; they make a wonderful addition to a ravioli filling.

Kofte samak Harissa mini fish cakes with preserved lemon

Serves 4–6

1 tablespoon olive oil

1 garlic clove, finely chopped

1 tablespoon coriander seeds, crushed

1 teaspoon paprika

500g (1lb 2oz) firm white fish fillets (such as
 hake, snapper, sea bream, or cod), skin
 and bones removed

rind of ½ preserved lemon, any pith
 removed and rind finely diced (see below)

4 spring onions, finely sliced

½ bunch of fresh coriander,
 roughly chopped

2 teaspoons harissa purée

1 egg

juice of ½ lemon

vegetable oil for frying

salt and freshly ground black pepper

These small fish cakes are full of flavours from Morocco and the North African coast. Harissa is a hot, fiery spice paste used across the Middle East. Preserved lemon is another ingredient that crops up in Moroccan cuisine, and it is easy to make yourself. An added bonus is that storing it under oil infuses that oil with a lemon flavour.

1 In a small pan, heat the olive oil and fry the garlic and coriander seeds until golden brown and fragrant. Add the paprika and remove from the heat.

2 Put the fish in a food processor with the aromatic fried spices, lemon rind, spring onion, and fresh coriander. Add the harissa and egg, and season with salt and pepper. Add half of the lemon juice and process until smooth.

3 Heat the vegetable oil in large frying pan over a medium-high heat. Fry a small piece of the mixture and taste to check the seasoning. Adjust with salt and black pepper, and an extra squeeze of fresh lemon juice if required. Roll the fish cakes into 16 portions. Fry the fish cakes in small batches until golden brown on all sides. Drain on kitchen paper.

4 Serve with a cucumber salad dressed with ground cinnamon and a little orange juice, or as a canapé with drinks before a meal.

Preserved lemons Place 2 lemons in a small tight-fitting pan. Cover with cold water. Add 3 heaped tablespoons sea salt (the salt removes the bitterness from the skin). Bring the water to the boil, and simmer for 10–12 minutes until the lemons are soft to the point of a knife. Remove from the hot water, and refresh under cold running water. When cool cut in half. Using a sharp knife, remove all the flesh and pith. Trim down the lemon skin from the inside, so you are just left with lozenges of lemon zest. Cover the lemon zest with olive oil and you have preserved lemon; it keeps covered in the refrigerator for up to 6 weeks.

Bolani Afghani flat bread

Makes 6–8

500g (1lb 2oz) plain flour

1 teaspoon salt

3 eggs, lightly beaten

150ml (5fl oz) olive oil plus extra for cooking

1 Sift the flour and salt into a bowl. Make a well in the centre, and add the eggs, olive oil, and 250ml (8fl oz) water. Bring together to make a ball of dough. Knead on a floured work surface for 10–15 minutes until very soft and elastic. Roll the dough into balls each roughly the size of a tennis ball. Cover with a damp cloth, and leave to rest for 30 minutes.

2 Oil the work surface and spread out one of the balls of dough, gently pulling the edges to stretch it as thin and wide as possible, as if you are making a strudel. Dust the surface with a little flour, and fold the pastry over and over to make a fan. Roll up this pleated piece of dough to make a curled ball. Repeat with the remaining balls of dough. Leave to rest for another 15 minutes.

3 Heat a heavy frying pan over a medium-high heat. Use your hands to pat a curled ball of dough into a circle 20cm (8in) in diameter. Add a little oil to the pan, and cook the flat disc of layered dough so that it is golden brown on each side. Repeat with the remaining balls of dough. Serve warm, accompanied by roast pumpkin paste (p154) and carrot pickle (p155).

Bolani is a delicious flaky flat bread. I spent a very enjoyable afternoon with a man called Billal in the Oakland Farmers' Market in San Francisco. His East West Gourmet company makes breads, relishes, and dips from his native Afghanistan. The recipes here and on pp154–5 are authentic street-food specials available at small stalls, cafés, and markets for generations. Every time I make this flat bread I think of Billal's generosity. When I asked for his card he just gave me another bag of flat bread, saying cheerily that it had his number on the front.

Kadu Roast pumpkin paste

Serves 6–8

1 sweet firm-fleshed pumpkin or butternut
   squash, about 1kg (2¼lb)

2 garlic cloves, finely chopped

1 tablespoon ground coriander

2 tablespoons olive oil

juice of ½ lemon

salt and freshly ground black pepper

This is one of the many dips I tasted at Billal's stall during my visit there (see p153). Roasting the pumpkin whole means that the roasted skin imparts its delicious nutty smoked flavour to the flesh inside. It is similar to roasting aubergine for baba ghanoush. Indeed, all the dips and relishes I tasted at Billal's stall were delicious, with a striking contrast between sweet and hot ingredients. There was a curried aubergine and tomato paste, and one made with spiced spinach. The spicy carrot pickle opposite worked best with the sweet pumpkin.

1 Roast the pumpkin whole in a preheated oven at 200°C (400°F/Gas 6) until soft and caramelized (40 minutes to an hour depending on the size). Do not make any cuts or incisions in the flesh because you will lose juice and flavour. Allow the pumpkin to cool, then cut in half. Scoop out the seeds and discard, then remove the soft cooked flesh and mash. Cut up about one-third of the cooked pumpkin skin. Finely chop, and mix with the pumpkin flesh.

2 Mix the garlic with the ground coriander. Heat a heavy pan and add the olive oil. Fry the garlic and coriander until fragrant. Add the cooked pumpkin and season well with salt and pepper. Add the lemon juice and taste. Adjust the seasoning as necessary. The flavours will be sweet and nutty, with a background of heat from the pepper, garlic, and coriander. The lemon juice provides the mixture with an edge and definition. The pumpkin flesh will be sweet and bland, and can take a lot of seasoning.

Turshi zardak Carrot pickle

Makes 4 large jars

1 tablespoon olive oil

6 garlic cloves, finely chopped

3 fresh red chillies, seeded and finely
  chopped

1 teaspoon cayenne pepper

2 teaspoons ground cumin

2 teaspoons ground coriander

1 teaspoon ground allspice

3kg (6½lb) carrots, peeled and finely grated

500g (1lb 2oz) sugar

500ml (16fl oz) malt vinegar

salt and freshly ground black pepper

1 Heat the oil in a large heavy pan over a medium-high heat for 2–3 minutes.
Add the garlic and chilli, and fry for a couple of minutes until fragrant.
Sprinkle in the cayenne pepper, cumin, coriander, and allspice. Cook for a further
minute or two. Add the carrot, sugar, and vinegar, and gently simmer over a low
heat for 40 minutes to 1 hour, or until the excess liquid has been cooked off and
the mixture is thick and syrupy. Season with salt and pepper. The mix should be
hot and spicy, but sweet with a pronounced sourness.

2 When it is ready, spoon the pickle into sterilized glass jars with tight-fitting
lids. Seal while the pickle is still hot, to create a vacuum. Allow at least
24 hours for the flavours to settle before using. It will keep in the same manner
as a chutney or relish if stored in a cool, dark place.

To enjoy a fantastic combination of flavours, take one of the hot bolani on p153, and spread with the roast pumpkin paste opposite. Add some houmous or a little yogurt. Spoon on the carrot pickle, then scatter with some fresh coriander leaves, roll it all up, and get stuck in. The combination of everything in one mouthful makes for a fantastic set of tastes. You could use pitta or naan bread to get great results as a snack. Treat this pickle like any chutney or relish. It can be put with cold meats or cheese, and complements just about anything it is paired with.

Fattoush Toasted pitta bread salad

Serves 4–6

2 large pitta breads, broken into pieces and
  toasted lightly

juice of about 1½ lemons

2 garlic cloves

4 ripe plum tomatoes, halved, seeded, and
  cut into 1cm (½in) dice

1 cucumber, halved, seeded, and cut into
  1cm (½in) dice

1 tablespoon ground sumac

4 spring onions, finely sliced

handful of fresh rocket leaves

½ bunch of fresh flat-leaf parsley leaves

½ bunch of fresh mint leaves

100ml (3½fl oz) extra virgin olive oil

salt and freshly ground black pepper

1 Place the toasted bread pieces in a large bowl. Add the juice of ½ lemon, and season well with salt and pepper.

2 Crush the garlic cloves with a little salt until you have a smooth purée. Mix the tomato and cucumber with the garlic purée. Season with salt and pepper, the sumac, and some more lemon juice. Mix the spring onion, rocket, parsley, and mint with the tomato mixture and olive oil. Add the toasted bread and some extra lemon juice.

3 Taste the salad. It should be sour from the lemon juice and peppery hot from the rocket and seasoning. The tomatoes and cucumber will be sweet, and the sumac is a grand spice that is purple in colour and provides an essential lemony, peppery element to the flavour of the salad. Serve immediately, as the lemon juice will start to eat into the leaves and discolour them.

Fattoush is a marvellous combination of simple flavours and textures that creates a result that is much more than the sum of its parts. Eaten at any time of day, it is often enjoyed as part of a mezze or accompanying grilled meat, kebabs, or chicken, or some fried falafel. It is a great way of using up stale pitta bread. The drier the bread, the more juice it absorbs. In Lebanese cooking lots of fresh herbs are used; this salad is no exception. Fresh and healthy, fattoush packs a tight punch for the taste buds. As a result it assumes near cult status with anyone who tries it.

Salatet kousa Courgette salad

Serves 4–6

1kg (2¼lb) small courgettes, ends trimmed (they should be not much longer than a man's index finger)

4 tablespoons extra virgin olive oil

1 garlic clove, crushed

2 teaspoons paprika

½ teaspoon ground cumin

½ teaspoon chilli powder

3 tablespoons lemon juice

30 fresh flat-leaf parsley leaves, roughly chopped

salt and freshly ground black pepper

This is a fresh and simple mezze-style dish which could accompany other vegetable dishes or meat or fish. When putting different dishes together, think about the dominant flavours present in each one, to avoid repetition. Colours and textures are also very important. Some dishes can be crisp and spicy; others could be a paste or a dip such as houmous or baba ghanoush. One could contain tahini; another could have roast almonds or pine nuts. Put them all together, and you have a colourful selection of dishes with variety in looks, ingredients, and tastes.

1 Cut the courgettes into quarters lengthways. (Do not use courgettes that are too thick because the inside will not be firm, but rather full of watery seeds.) Alternatively, you could cut the outside flesh away from the central core of the courgette and discard the seeds.

2 Heat a heavy frying pan over a medium-high heat. Add a little oil and fry the courgette in batches until golden brown on two sides. Cooking in batches helps to ensure that the temperature of the pan does not drop, which would result in the vegetables steaming or boiling in their own juices. Also, do not overcook, otherwise the courgette will be soggy.

3 Meanwhile, crush the garlic with a little salt and combine with the spices, the remaining olive oil, and the lemon juice. Place the cooked courgette in a bowl, and cover with the dressing. Leave for 1 hour before serving. Taste and adjust the seasoning where appropriate, then garnish with the parsley. Serve with grilled meat or fish, or as part of a selection of mezze to start the meal.

Salatet semsum Sesame salad

Serves 6 as part of a mezze

1 garlic clove

large pinch of sea salt

100ml (3½fl oz) tahini

1 tablespoon white vinegar

3 cucumbers, cut into small cubes

4 spring onions, finely sliced

30 fresh flat-leaf parsley leaves, chopped

½ teaspoon coarse-ground black pepper

3 tablespoons extra virgin olive oil

juice of ½ lemon

2 tablespoons sesame seeds, toasted

1 Crush the garlic with the salt until smooth. Add the tahini, and stir in the white vinegar until the mixture reaches a consistency like yogurt. Stir in the cucumber, parsley, and pepper. Add the remaining olive oil and the lemon juice.

2 Serve alongside kofte kebab (see pp176–7) or grilled chicken, garnished with the toasted sesame seeds.

Mezze is a great way to start a meal, and there are hundreds of variations of little dishes that can be served with olives, pickles, and lots of hot bread. Tahini is a very important ingredient in the Middle East. This paste made from sesame seeds is present in houmous and a sauce called tarator (see p185). Mezze is often eaten at a small café or stall with friends, before going to eat at home with family. The idea with this style of eating is that it is a collection of flavours and textures in different dishes. Eaten together, they complement and contrast with each other.

Dzhazh garfa pilaf bil iluz Eastern
jewelled pilaf with cinnamon and almonds

This juicy and aromatic chicken dish is jewelled with shining fried raisins, chopped dates, almonds, and onions flecked with strands of saffron. The succulent dried fruits and colourful, fragrant spices create an image of the exotic East, a land of jewels, silks, and mystique. I enjoyed many variations of this in Jordan and Turkey. It can be eaten hot or cold, and is visually striking because of the caramelized onions and bright orange turmeric and saffron. It could be made using baby chickens, partridge, or quail, allowing a small bird per person.

Serves 8

60ml (2fl oz) olive oil	½ teaspoon ground turmeric
3 cinnamon sticks	½ teaspoon ground cinnamon
6 green cardamom pods	¼ teaspoon ground cardamom
10 black peppercorns	20g (¾oz) butter
3 onions, finely chopped	100g (3½oz) almonds
200ml (7fl oz) tomato juice	100g (3½oz) raisins
2 medium chickens, each jointed into	50g (1¾oz) chopped dates
at least 4 pieces	½ teaspoon saffron threads
600g (1lb 5oz) rice, rinsed	salt and freshly ground black pepper

1 Preheat the overhead grill until medium-hot. Heat a heavy pan over a medium-high heat, and add 1 tablespoon of the olive oil. Add the whole spices – cinnamon sticks, cardamom pods, and peppercorns – and fry for a couple of minutes until aromatic. Add about one-third of the onion, and cook until soft and pale golden. Add the tomato juice and 1 litre (1¾ pints) water, season with salt, and bring to the boil. Reduce the heat to a gentle simmer and add the chicken pieces; cook gently for about 10 minutes. Remove the chicken from the broth, sprinkle the chicken with half the ground spices, and set aside.

2 Pour the rice into the broth. Cook over a high heat until the liquid is almost absorbed, then over a low heat until cooked. Remove from the heat and leave covered until needed.

3 Place the chicken on an oven tray, and cook under the overhead grill until golden brown all over. In a separate pan, melt half the butter and fry the almonds until golden brown. Remove from the pan, and fry the raisins and dates. Add to the almonds. Melt the remaining butter, and fry the remaining onion until golden brown. Add the rest of the ground spices and the saffron to the onion. Taste and adjust the seasoning with salt and pepper.

4 To serve, stir the onion mixture into the rice with half the almond and fruit mixture. Place the rice in a dish with the chicken pieces on top. Scatter the remaining almond and fruit mixture over the top.

Kebab b'il karaz

Lamb meatballs with sour cherry sauce

Serves 6–8

300g (10oz) pitted dried sour cherries

1 tablespoon sugar

1 tablespoon pomegranate molasses

juice of 1 lemon

For the meatballs

2 garlic cloves, halved and any green inner
    stem removed

2 small dried red chillies, finely chopped

2 teaspoons ground coriander

pinch of salt

a little olive oil

1 onion, finely chopped

500g (1lb 2oz) lamb mince

½ bunch of fresh flat-leaf parsley,
    roughly chopped

freshly ground black pepper

1   Put the dried cherries in a heavy pan. Add 200ml (7fl oz) water and the sugar and pomegranate molasses. Bring to the boil, then reduce the heat and gently simmer for 30 minutes until the sauce is thick and syrupy. When reduced, add the lemon juice and taste, adjusting the seasoning if necessary (bearing in mind that the meatballs will be salty, rich, and peppery hot).

2   Meanwhile, make the meatballs. Crush the garlic, dried chilli, and ground coriander with a pinch of salt to make a paste. Heat a heavy pan over a medium-high heat and add a little olive oil. Fry the paste for about 2 minutes until fragrant. Add the onion and sauté quickly for 4 minutes. Remove from the heat, and transfer the onion mixture to a bowl with the lamb. Add the parsley and season well with salt and pepper. Roll the meat into small balls about the size of cherry tomatoes.

3   Heat a clean heavy pan over a medium-high heat. Add a little olive oil, and fry the meatballs in small batches until golden brown all over. Drain on kitchen paper. Add the meatballs to the cherry sauce. Cook for a couple of minutes to combine the flavours. Serve as part of a main course, as one of many dishes of simple grilled and marinated meats, vegetables, and lots of bread.

Sour cherries The fresh sour cherries that are traditionally used for this dish are of such good quality that they are a bit difficult to come by unless you have a good Persian, Iranian, Turkish, or Lebanese grocer nearby. Dried sour cherries make a perfect substitute and are available from supermarkets.

This dish is an unusually striking combination of flavours that makes your taste buds tingle. It works well with something quite neutral in taste because it is very rich. It hails from an area of Turkey in the south, near the Aleppo region in Syria. I have had variations of this in both Turkey and Syria. When I first had these meatballs, they came at the end of a vast meal, yet room was made on the table and in our stomachs. The sizzling serving dish was scraped clean, and the extra sauce mopped up with copious amounts of flat bread.

Fatayer bisabanikh Spinach pastries

Makes 25–30 pastries

For the pastry

30g (1oz) fresh yeast or 15g (½oz) dried

450g (1lb) plain flour

1 teaspoon salt

2 tablespoons olive oil

For the filling

900g (2lb) spinach, stems discarded,
  rinsed, and drained in a colander

1 pomegranate

3 tablespoons olive oil

1 onion, finely grated or very finely chopped

2 garlic cloves, finely chopped

100g (3½oz) pine nuts

100g (3½oz) walnuts

1 teaspoon ground sumac (optional)

juice of 1½ lemons

salt and freshly ground black pepper

These triangular pastries have remained unchanged for centuries. Variations of this would have been made in the Levant region at the time of the crusades. In the days when everyone baked their own bread, the home cook would make enough dough for the whole week's worth of bread and these savoury pastries. Fillings vary hugely from spinach or chard, to cheese, mushroom, or spiced lamb, and can be spiked with spices or be quite plain. The same dough is used for small crescent-shaped pastries called "samboosak", which are often fried; the triangular ones are baked.

1 To make the pastry, mix the yeast in a jug with a spoonful of the flour and a small amount of water to make a paste. Stir in 150ml (5fl oz) lukewarm water, and leave in a warm place for 10 minutes. Sift the flour and salt into a large bowl. Make a well in the centre, add the oil and yeast mixture, and mix together. Gradually add another 150ml (5fl oz) lukewarm water until incorporated. Turn the dough onto a floured surface. Knead for 15 minutes until shiny and elastic. Form into a ball, and place in a lightly oiled large bowl. Cover with cling film or a clean cloth. Leave to rise in a warm place for about 2 hours until it doubles in size.

2 Chop the spinach leaves and squeeze dry. Remove the seeds from the pomegranate (see tip on p36), and put in a bowl with the juice. Heat the oil in a heavy pan over a medium heat. Add the onion and sweat for 3–4 minutes until soft. Push to one side of the pan. Add the garlic, pine nuts, and walnuts. Increase the heat and fry the garlic and nuts until golden brown. Mix the nuts into the onion mixture, and reduce the heat. Add the spinach and cook for 2–3 minutes until wilted. Add the sumac (if using), pomegranate seeds, and lemon juice. Check the seasoning. Remove from the heat and set aside.

3 Preheat the oven to 190°C (375°F/Gas 5). Break the dough into 25–30 equal-sized balls. Roll into thin discs on a floured work surface. Put a teaspoon of filling in the centre of each disc (don't include too much liquid). Bring up the sides of the dough to form a three-sided packet, pinch the edges together firmly, and place on an oiled baking tray. Bake in the oven for 5 minutes, then reduce the temperature to 180°C (350°F/Gas 4). Bake for a further 15 minutes.

Harira Spicy bean soup

Serves 6

100g (3½oz) dried chickpeas

100g (3½oz) dried cannellini beans or fava
  beans or butter beans

100g (3½oz) dried split green peas

1 teaspoon bicarbonate of soda

1 tablespoon coriander seeds

1 tablespoon cumin seeds

2 small dried chillies

1 teaspoon ground cloves

½ teaspoon cayenne pepper

4cm (1¾in) piece of fresh root
  ginger, grated

3 garlic cloves olive oil for cooking

1 cinnamon stick

3 onions, finely chopped

8 ripe tomatoes, coarsely grated
  (see tip in method on p173)

100g (3½oz) red or yellow lentils, picked
  and rinsed

juice of 1 lemon plus a little extra to finish

½ bunch of fresh coriander, leaves picked
  and roughly chopped

salt and freshly ground black pepper

*During the Muslim fast
of Ramadam, you are
allowed to eat only after
the sun has gone down,
and you also eat little or
no meat. As a result there
are lots of substantial
vegetarian dishes, such as
this bean soup, that are
sold at the food stalls and
in the night markets after
the sun has set. You can use
any combination of dried
beans, lentils, or chickpeas
for this hearty soup, as well
as different blends of spices.
The flavours improve over
24 hours, blending and
softening. Serve with a
spoon of cooling yogurt in
the centre of each bowl and
lots of fresh crusty bread.*

1 Soak the chickpeas and cannellini beans overnight in plenty of cold water. The split green peas need only be soaked for 2 hours. Drain and rinse the chickpeas and beans. Put in a large pan, cover with lots of cold water, and add the bicarbonate of soda. Bring to the boil over a medium heat. Reduce the heat and simmer for 40–60 minutes until the beans are cooked, but not mushy. Skim off any scum or impurities with a ladle as they are simmering. Drain and rinse.

2 Meanwhile, using a pestle and mortar, grind the coriander seeds, cumin seeds, and dried chilli to a fine powder. Add the cloves, cayenne pepper, ginger, and garlic, and work into a paste. Heat 2 tablespoons oil in a heavy pan over a medium-high heat. Add the spice mixture and cinnamon stick. Fry for 2 minutes until fragrant. Reduce the heat, add the onion, and sweat for about 10 minutes until the onion starts to caramelize. Add the tomato pulp; cook until any excess liquid has evaporated. Rinse the split green peas, add to the tomato mixture with the lentils, and stir through. Add 2 litres (3½ pints) water, bring to the boil, reduce the heat, and simmer for 20 minutes. Add the rinsed chickpeas and beans. Mix together. Season well and add the lemon juice and half the coriander. Leave the soup off the heat for 5 minutes, then check the seasoning.

3 To serve, garnish with the remaining coriander and a little extra squeeze of lemon juice. This soup can be eaten hot or warm at any time of the year.

Baba ghanoush
Smoky roast aubergine dip

This classic Lebanese aubergine dip is the perfect accompaniment to cheese, salad, or grilled meat. It works particularly well with the smoky rich flavours of rare grilled beef or lamb. I have made this recipe slightly smoother and richer by adding crème fraîche; yogurt could be added instead. Throughout my travels in the Middle East I never tired of this delicious dip, eaten with lots of freshly baked bread. Once you make some yourself, you will never again be satisfied with the shop-bought version.

Serves 4–6

3 aubergines
2 garlic cloves, finely chopped
pinch of salt
1 tablespoon tahini
½ teaspoon cayenne pepper

juice of ½ lemon
100ml (3½fl oz) extra virgin olive oil
2 tablespoons crème fraîche
  or Greek-style yogurt
freshly ground black pepper

1 Place the aubergines either directly on a preheated hot plate (electric or gas fire) or under a very hot overhead grill. Roast the aubergines for 10–12 minutes until the skin is blistered and charred on all sides. Keep turning the aubergines using tongs while they are cooking. Remove from the heat and place in a bowl. Cover with cling film and allow to cool. As the aubergines cool steam is trapped, which in turn continues to cook the aubergines and helps to loosen the charred skin. When the aubergines are cool, remove from the bowl and pull away the softened blackened skin. Scoop out the cooked aubergine flesh using a spoon (the skin is discarded).

2 Crush the garlic with a pinch of salt. Put the garlic and aubergine flesh into the food processor. Add the tahini and season with the cayenne, salt, and pepper. Work until smooth, then add the lemon juice. With the motor running, gradually add the olive oil in a thin, steady stream to make a paste (similar to making mayonnaise). When it is all combined, stir in the crème fraîche.

3 Check the seasoning. There should be a smoky sweetness from the roasted aubergine, while the tahini and salt provide a savoury component. The lemon juice and crème fraîche are sour, and the black pepper is hot and peppery. Adjust the seasoning as necessary. Serve in a bowl as an accompaniment to other dishes, or as a dip with lots of fresh bread.

Labneh Yogurt cream cheese dip

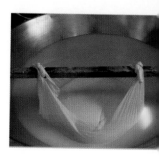

Serves 8 as a dip or part of a mezze

1 litre (1¾ pints) goat's or
   sheep's milk yogurt

1 teaspoon salt

1 tablespoon olive oil

paprika or ground cumin, to garnish

1   Put the yogurt in a bowl with the salt. Whisk together to combine thoroughly. Place a colander in the sink, and line with a clean fine-weave wet cloth such as muslin or cheesecloth, or even a new finely woven dishcloth. Pour in the yogurt, and tie the corners of the cloth around the tap. Allow the liquid to drain from the cloth for about 12 hours or overnight.

2   To serve, transfer to a serving bowl, mix the olive oil with the labneh, and scatter a little paprika or cumin over the top as a garnish. Enjoy as a dip with lots of fresh bread or as one of a number of dishes served mezze-style. Don't be deceived by the simple recipe and method; the flavour of the yogurt is completely transformed.

Labneh is an essential taste of the Middle East. It is eaten in many guises at all times of the day, as a snack or part of a whole meal. Although labneh is traditionally made from goat's milk yogurt, Greek sheep's milk yogurt is a great substitute. It is very popular as a mezze-style dip eaten with kofte kebabs (see pp176–7) or falafel. Labneh is delicious plain or can be flavoured with crushed garlic, chopped chilli, ground cumin or paprika, or some freshly chopped mint. It can be made into a more substantial dip by adding chopped cucumber, or spring onion and tomato.

Shlada al falfla hamra al khizzou

Carrot and orange salad with
paprika dressing

This is a deliciously simple
and effective salad that
I had at a small stall in
Marrakesh. Some grilled
chicken marinated with
harissa accompanied it.
This salad has got so much
going on in the dressing,
and yet all your taste buds
are stimulated in unison.
There are also lots of
different textures. The
juicy oranges contrast with
the crisp carrot and
crunchy sesame seeds. Serve
with simple grilled and
roasted meats, or with
something more complex.
It can be a small part of
a larger collection of dishes,
and makes a good addition
to a barbecue or picnic.

Serves 4–6

3 tablespoons sesame seeds

3 or 4 generous handfuls of rocket
  or lettuce leaves

500g (1lb 2oz) carrots, peeled and grated

2 oranges, peeled, pith removed, and flesh
  cut into segments

juice of 1 lemon

30 fresh flat-leaf parsley leaves,
  roughly chopped

salt and freshly ground black pepper

Paprika dressing

1 teaspoon honey

¼ teaspoon salt

1 tablespoon water

½ teaspoon paprika

1 teaspoon mustard

60ml (2fl oz) extra virgin olive oil

1 tablespoon red wine vinegar

freshly ground black pepper

1 Roast the sesame seeds in a dry frying pan over a medium-high heat for
a few minutes; take care they do not scorch. Remove from the heat.

2 Arrange the rocket in a bowl with the carrot and orange segments. Season
with salt and pepper. Squeeze the lemon juice over the top, and scatter with
the flat-leaf parsley.

3 Put all the ingredients for the dressing in a glass jar with a secure-fitting lid,
add 1 tablespoon water, and shake to combine thoroughly. Pour over the
top of the carrot salad, and garnish with the toasted sesame seeds.

Lahem bil ajine Lebanese lamb pizza

Makes 15–20

1 quantity of yeast dough (see p164),
   kneaded until elastic and shiny

2 tablespoons olive oil

4 onions, finely chopped

8 large plum tomatoes

500g (1lb 2oz) lamb mince

2 teaspoons ground coriander

1 teaspoon Lebanese spice mix (see p218)

1 tablespoon tomato purée

1 tablespoon pomegranate molasses

1 teaspoon soft brown sugar

100g (3½oz) pine nuts

small handful of fresh coriander,
   roughly chopped

small handful of fresh flat-leaf parsley,
   roughly chopped

salt and freshly ground black pepper

Greek-style yogurt or tahini,
   to serve (optional)

lemon wedges, to serve (optional)

1 Prepare the dough following the instructions on p164. To make the topping, heat the oil in a heavy frying pan over a medium-high heat. Add the onion and sweat over a brisk heat for 4 minutes until soft but without too much colour.

2 Meanwhile, cut the tomatoes in half. Hold one of the tomato halves with the skin side in the palm of your hand. Using a large grater, grate the flesh of the tomato. (This is a great way of making tomato pulp without having to blanch and peel the tomatoes; the skin stays in your hand to be discarded.) Set aside.

3 Add the lamb to the onion mixture, and sauté for 4–5 minutes until browned and broken up. Season with the spices and a good amount of salt and pepper. Add the grated tomato pulp, tomato purée, pomegranate molasses, and sugar. Cook for another 5 minutes or until any liquid has evaporated. Stir in the pine nuts, coriander and parsley. Taste the mixture and adjust the seasoning to suit your taste. Remove from the heat, and allow the mixture to cool.

4 While the mixture is cooling, preheat the oven to 220°C (425°F/Gas 7). Break the dough into 15–20 equal-sized balls. Roll each ball into rounds or oval shapes on a floured work surface. Lightly spread the meat and pine nut filling onto the rolled pastry, leaving a border around the edge. Place the pizzas on an oiled baking tray, and bake in the oven for 12–15 minutes until the pastry is crisp and golden. Serve immediately, with a little yogurt or tahini spooned over the top, or served with a wedge of lemon (if using).

These are a delicious floppy sort of pizza or open-faced pie. Lamb is traditionally used, but you could also use minced beef. You could also make a vegetarian version with lots of sautéed mushrooms. Much smaller in size than an Italian pizza, you would generally buy a few of these to be eaten on the go. They are baked in wood ovens in bakeries and roadside cafés from Istanbul to Beirut and Damascus, and everywhere in between. Some versions are spicy, while others are a little subtler. The pomegranate molasses used here adds great depth of flavour to the meat.

Qesbur sharmula hut
Coriander marinated fish

From Turkey to Morocco, the people of the countries bordering the Eastern and Southern Mediterranean eat a great deal of fish, often cooked whole. Freshly cooked fish is a very popular dish at street stalls and markets. Often the ovens, grills, and hot charcoal are only yards from the fish markets, or the water's edge itself. This simple recipe can be used for any whole fish, whatever the size. It works just as well with a sea bass or snapper, fresh-caught mackerel or plump sardines, or portions of fish. It can be served as the centrepiece of a large summer barbecue or buffet.

Serves 4–6

1 large white firm-fleshed fish such as bass, snapper, or sea bream, about 2kg (4½lb)
3 garlic cloves, finely chopped
1 teaspoon ground coriander
1 teaspoon ground cumin
3 tablespoons olive oil
100g (3½oz) onion, finely chopped

3 tomatoes, roughly diced
2 fresh green chillies, deseeded and finely chopped
1 bunch of fresh coriander, leaves picked and roughly chopped
4 lemons
sea salt and freshly ground black pepper

1   Preheat the oven to 200°C (400°F/Gas 6). Clean the inside of the fish and season with salt and pepper, a little of the garlic, and some of the spices. Rub inside and out. Heat a heavy pan over a medium-high heat and add a little oil. Fry the fish quickly on both sides until golden brown. Carefully lift from the pan and place in an ovenproof dish.

2   Add a little extra oil to the same pan, and fry the remaining garlic and spices. Add the onion and tomato. Add most of the chopped coriander, the green chilli, and the juice of 3 of the lemons. Cook for 3–4 minutes. Stuff the fish with the onion mixture; spoon any remaining mixture over the fish. Cover with foil and bake in the oven for 20–25 minutes until cooked, depending on the size of the fish. To check, insert a fork into the dense meat at the back of the head. If the meat is white and flaky, the fish is done. (Remember, when a piece of fish or meat is taken from the oven, it will continue to cook from the residual heat.)

3   To serve, garnish with the remaining chopped coriander and the juice of the final lemon. The spices, green chilli, and lemon work together to cut the rich fattiness of the fish. This dish is delicious whether eaten hot, warm, or cold, accompanied by freshly cooked vegetables and salads, and freshly made bread.

Kofte kebab Lamb kebabs with white bean and tomato salad

I had this fantastic variation of a spicy kofte, or kofte kebab, in the spring in Istanbul. I ate them in view of the mighty Bosphorus. The rich, juicy meat was very well spiced with cumin and paprika, and studded throughout with bright green pistachio nuts. When you cut into the meat they glistened like shining jewels. The kebabs here are smaller than the traditional long kofte kebab, so you may need to cut down the bamboo skewers to size. Or simply make as small meatballs if you prefer, flattening them slightly once in the pan.

Serves 4–6

2 garlic cloves, halved

a little olive oil

1 onion, finely chopped

2 teaspoons ground cumin

2 teaspoons paprika

1 teaspoon cayenne pepper

500g (1lb 2oz) lamb mince

handful of fresh flat-leaf parsley, leaves
   picked and roughly chopped

handful of fresh coriander, leaves picked
   and roughly chopped

100g (3½oz) unsalted pistachio nuts,
   roughly chopped

sea salt and freshly ground black pepper

For the salad

300g (10oz) dried cannellini beans

2 garlic cloves, peeled but left whole

½ bunch of fresh flat-leaf parsley, leaves
   picked and chopped (stalks reserved)

3 tablespoons red wine vinegar

3 tablespoons extra virgin olive oil

1 teaspoon ground cumin

2 ripe tomatoes, cut into 1cm (½in) dice

1 To make the salad, soak the beans overnight in a large bowl of cold water. Drain and rinse under cold running water. Put into a large heavy pan, and cover with fresh cold water. Add the garlic, reserved parsley stalks, and a splash of olive oil. Do not add salt. Bring to the boil, reduce the heat, and simmer for 1 hour 20 minutes to 1 hour 40 minutes until the beans are soft with a bit of bite. Drain off the liquid. Add the vinegar, extra virgin olive oil, and cumin to the beans, and stir through. Season well with salt and pepper. Leave for about 20 minutes to absorb all the flavours. Add the tomato and parsley just before serving.

2 To make the kebabs, soak the bamboo skewers in cold water for at least 30 minutes so they do not burn. Crush the garlic with a little salt to make a paste. Heat a little oil in a heavy pan over a medium-high heat. Fry the onion for 4 minutes until soft. Add the garlic, cumin, paprika, and cayenne, and fry for a couple of minutes until aromatic. Remove from the heat, transfer to a bowl, and leave to cool for 5 minutes. Add the mince, parsley, coriander, and pistachio nuts. Season well. Mould the lamb mixture onto one end of the skewer, making a cylinder of meat around roughly half its length. Heat a little oil in a heavy pan over a medium-high heat. Fry the kofte kebabs in batches until golden brown all over. Drain on kitchen paper. Serve with the salad and lots of fresh crusty bread.

Salatet bil s'banegh joz
Spinach and walnut salad

Serves 4–6

2 tablespoons extra virgin olive oil

1 onion, finely chopped

250g (9oz) fresh spinach, rinsed, stems
   discarded, and leaves roughly chopped

30g (1oz) walnuts

1 garlic clove, finely chopped

150ml (5fl oz) Greek-style yogurt

20 fresh mint leaves,
   roughly chopped

seeds of ½ pomegranate
   (see method on p36)

salt and freshly ground black pepper

1 Heat the olive oil in a heavy pan over a medium-high heat, and fry the
   onion for 4–5 minutes until pale golden. Add the spinach and wilt down for
a couple of minutes. Remove from the heat. In a separate pan, dry-roast the
walnuts over a medium-high heat for a few minutes, then roughly chop. Crush
the garlic with a little salt and add to the yogurt.

2 Season the spinach with salt and black pepper. Drain off any excess liquid
   and place on a serving dish. Pour over the yogurt and garlic mixture. Scatter
over the walnuts and mint, and garnish with the pomegranate seeds.

This is another deliciously
simple mezze that could be
eaten at the beginning of
the meal with other dishes.
What often happens when
eating in this way in the
Middle East is that the
small dishes and plates stay
on the table, even when the
next course of meat arrives.
It is a seamless, continuous
flow of food arriving at the
table. This is a perfect
combination of flavours
and textures – the sourness
of pomegranate and yogurt
complement the earthy
flavour of the walnuts.
It could also be served as
a salad on its own or
accompanying some grilled
meat, fish, or chicken.

Lohz Spiced roast almonds

Serves 6–8 with drinks

3 tablespoons sunflower oil

275g (10oz) whole blanched almonds

1 teaspoon ground cumin

1 teaspoon ground cinnamon

½ teaspoon ground chilli flakes

85g (3oz) soft brown sugar

juice of ½ lemon

salt and freshly ground black pepper

Nuts and seeds feature in many dishes throughout the Levant and along the North African coast, from mezze and snacks, to main courses and desserts. With each nut stall or trader come family recipes and spice mixes passed down over generations. In the scented passages of the souk in Damascus I happened upon an ingenious portable nut stall that was a customized bicycle. At the front where a basket would have been was a flat hotplate heated underneath with charcoal. This ensured that the nuts were freshly roasted in small batches. The bike came complete with a six-foot metal chimney.

1 Preheat the oven to 150°C (300°F/Gas 2). Heat a heavy frying pan over a medium-high heat. Add the oil, almonds, cumin, cinnamon, chilli, and two-thirds of the soft brown sugar. Toss the nuts in the sugar to coat thoroughly. Continue to sauté until the nuts are caramelized and all the sugar has melted. Add the lemon juice and stir through.

2 Transfer the nuts to a bowl, and season well with salt and pepper. Stir through to mix together. Spread the nuts on a baking tray, and roast in the oven for 5 minutes, to allow them to dry out. Sprinkle with the remaining brown sugar to taste.

3 Serve warm or at room temperature. They will keep in a clean, dry airtight container for a couple of weeks without spoiling.

Grinding and refreshing spices Grinding your own spices from whole pods and seeds is so simple it is worth making this a habit. The reward far outweighs any extra time and effort involved, as freshly ground spices have much better flavour and aroma than store-bought versions do. Invest in an electric coffee grinder or a wooden one that has a small drawer. Grind a batch as small or as large as you want, then sieve to get rid of any tough husks. (Don't make too large a batch if you are not going to be using it within a relatively short period of time, as it will only become stale.) Store the spice mixture in an airtight jar with a screwtop lid, and use as needed. To refresh ground spices, place the quantity that you want to use in a dry frying pan, and heat over a low-medium heat for a couple of minutes until the spice becomes fragrant.

Kara'a Libyan pumpkin dip

Serves 6

500g (1lb 2oz) pumpkin, peeled, deseeded, and flesh cut into 2cm (1in) cubes

1 teaspoon caraway seeds

1 teaspoon cumin seeds

3 garlic cloves, finely chopped

1 fresh red chilli, deseeded and finely chopped

juice of 1 lemon

60–100ml (2–3½fl oz) extra virgin olive oil

salt and freshly ground black pepper

1 Put the pumpkin in a saucepan with 150ml (5fl oz) water, and simmer for about 10 minutes until soft. Season well with salt and pepper. Mash the pumpkin with a fork until smooth. Set aside.

2 Dry-roast the caraway and cumin seeds in a small frying pan over a medium-high heat for a couple of minutes until aromatic. Crush the toasted seeds using a pestle and mortar. Add the garlic, chilli, and a pinch of salt, and work into a smooth paste. Add the spice mixture to the pumpkin with the lemon juice. Mix through, then stir in the olive oil. Serve either hot or cold as part of a mezze, accompanied by lots of hot pitta bread.

Throughout the Middle East, dips and pastes are eaten as part of a larger selection of mezze. Lots of them are vegetable-based, a light and healthy option compared to the often richer meat-based main courses. This dip makes a change from some of the more common ones such as houmous. The chilli and spices provide a peppery heat, contrasting with the pumpkin's sweetness. Try butternut squash, sweet potato, or beetroot in place of the pumpkin. The vegetables could also be roasted, then puréed, to give added depth of flavour to the finished dip.

Muhammara Spiced tomato relish

Serves 6–8

2 red peppers

100g (3½oz) walnuts

100g (3½oz) hazelnuts

10 cherry tomatoes, halved

1 fresh red chilli, deseeded and
  finely chopped

2 garlic cloves, halved

1 teaspoon cayenne pepper

1 teaspoon ground cumin

1 tablespoon pomegranate molasses

100ml (3½fl oz) olive oil

juice of 1 lemon

I had similar pastes to this in Syria, Turkey, and Lebanon. They are left on the table so that they can accompany soups and grilled meats. In Turkey and Syria, this spicy red sauce is called "muhammara", which means "made red". Some pastes contain walnuts; others use roast hazelnuts. Red peppers or tomatoes, or both, can be made to sweeten the paste and bulk it out. However it is made, this paste is packed with spicy fire and is addictively delicious. It works particularly well when the flavours are allowed to develop overnight or even a few days.

1 Heat a griddle pan or overhead grill until very hot. Grill the pepper until the skin is blistered and charred on all sides. Transfer to a bowl and cover tightly with cling film. The trapped moisture makes it easier to peel off the blackened skin. Once cooled slightly, halve and remove any seeds and membrane, then peel and discard the skin. Roughly chop the flesh.

2 Process the walnuts and hazelnuts in a food processor until finely ground. Add the pepper, tomato, chilli, garlic, cayenne, cumin, and pomegranate molasses. Work into a smooth paste. With the motor running, gradually add the oil in a steady stream, as if you were making a mayonnaise. If the mixture gets too thick, add a little of the lemon juice. Once the oil has all been incorporated, add the remaining lemon juice and combine.

3 Serve at room temperature as a dip with lots of hot fresh pitta bread, or as one of many dishes as part of a mezze selection. If not serving straight away, store in the refrigerator until needed. It will keep up to 5 days, and over that time the flavour will only become more intense.

Tarator bi tahini Sesame tarator sauce

Serves 6 as part of a mezze selection

2 garlic cloves

½ teaspoon salt

large pinch of cayenne pepper

250ml (8fl oz) tahini

100ml (3½oz) good-quality olive oil

150ml (5fl oz) fresh lemon juice

salt and freshly ground black pepper

1 Crush the garlic cloves using the back of a heavy knife on a board. Add the salt and cayenne pepper. Continue to work until you have a smooth paste.

2 Transfer the garlic paste to a bowl, and whisk continuously while slowly pouring in the tahini and olive oil, as if you were making a mayonnaise. If the mixture gets too thick, thin with a little lemon juice, then continue the process. Once all the tahini and olive oil have been incorporated, add the remaining lemon juice. Taste the sauce and season with a little salt and pepper if necessary.

Note If the nut flavour is too overpowering, try whisking a little yogurt into the mixture, which softens the intensity.

Tarator bi sonoba (pine nut tarator sauce) Remove the crust from 2 slices of white bread. Soak the bread in a little milk until soft. Crush 2 peeled garlic cloves using the back of a heavy knife on a board. Add ½ teaspoon salt and a large pinch of cayenne pepper. Work until smooth. Place the paste in a food processor with 225g (8oz) pine nuts and work until fine. Add the soaked bread and any excess milk. Continue to process, gradually adding 100ml (3½fl oz) oil in a steady stream, as if you were making a mayonnaise. Thin the sauce with the juice of 2 lemons. Taste and season with salt and freshly ground black pepper. This delicious sauce complements grilled meat, fish, and vegetables. You could use a combination of nuts such as almonds or walnuts to get a more complex depth of flavour, or roast some of them before grinding to create more contrast.

This sauce is used often in Middle Eastern food, served with hot and cold vegetable dishes, as well as falafel or as part of a mezze table. It is most often served cold; however, in one small market café by the coast in Lebanon, I had a delicious dish where fresh firm fillets of white fish were first grilled, then coated in this tahini sauce with lots of chopped parsley, and finally baked in the oven. The sweet fresh fish was a great contrast to the intense lemony, nutty sauce. Another version, tarator bi sonoba, is made with pine nuts; the recipe for this is also given.

Ablama Courgettes stuffed with lamb and pine nuts

I had these delicious spiced courgettes in a small café in Damascus in Syria. They are definitely worth the bit of fuss that is needed to make them. The key is to get small firm courgettes at the beginning of the season, as opposed to massive watery ones that are mostly seeds inside. There is an alternative preparation method. Simply cut the courgettes in half lengthways, then scrape all the seeds out using a small spoon. Each half is then stuffed with the filling. The courgettes are still fried, but you do not turn them over; otherwise the meat stuffing will fall out!

Serves 6

1kg (2¼lb) small courgettes

100ml (3½fl oz) olive oil

2 garlic cloves, finely chopped

½ teaspoon ground cumin

½ teaspoon ground cloves

½ teaspoon ground cinnamon

1 onion, finely chopped

600g (1lb 5oz) lamb mince

100g (3½oz) pine nuts

3 ripe tomatoes

30 flat-leaf parsley leaves, roughly chopped

juice of 1 lemon

200ml (7fl oz) good-quality chicken stock

salt and freshly ground black pepper

1 Cut the tops off the courgettes and, using a small spoon, hollow out the inside of each courgette.

2 Heat 1 tablespoon of the olive oil in a heavy pan over a medium-high heat. Fry the garlic, cumin, cloves, and cinnamon for a couple of minutes until fragrant. Add the onion and cook until soft and pale golden, then add the lamb. Keep cooking until all the liquid has evaporated, stirring the lamb around the pan to prevent it becoming lumpy. Season well with salt and pepper. Add the pine nuts and mix well. Taste the mixture and adjust the seasoning.

3 Cut a cross in the bottom of the tomatoes and, using the point of a small knife, remove the core of each one. Blanch in boiling water for 10 seconds, then refresh in cold water. Peel off the skin and discard. Cut the tomatoes in half, remove the seeds, and cut the flesh into small dice. Set aside.

4 Using a small spoon, stuff the courgettes with the lamb mixture, pushing the filling down into each courgette so that it is plump with stuffing. Heat the remaining oil, and fry the courgettes until soft. Cook in batches while continuing to stuff the remainder of the courgettes.

5 Mix the diced tomato with the parsley, and season with salt and pepper. Add the lemon juice and chicken stock. Place the cooked courgettes in a flameproof dish. Pour the tomato mixture over the top, and cook over a medium heat until the sauce is hot. Serve with rice or bread. This dish works particularly well with a selection of other mezze dishes, with lots of hot bread to soak up all the good cooking juices.

Houmous bil erfeh lahem
Houmous with cinnamon lamb

This is a fresh version of houmous without the strong flavour of the sesame that comes from the tahini. There are a number of variations of houmous: some are smooth; others have a rougher texture. This one uses dried chilli and cayenne pepper to give a great warmth that works very well with the fried lamb and the other spices. Alternatively, leave out the spices and add lots of freshly chopped parsley and coriander instead. It can be served without the fried lamb, but this combination is typical of the small cafés in Beirut and Lebanon.

Serves 6

2 garlic cloves

¼ teaspoon ground dried chilli flakes

425g (15oz) can cooked chickpeas, drained and rinsed

2 tablespoons extra virgin olive oil

½ teaspoon cayenne pepper

small handful of fresh flat-leaf parsley, plus extra, roughly chopped, to garnish

3 tablespoons lemon juice

1 tablespoon Greek-style yogurt

2 tablespoons sunflower oil

100g (3½oz) lamb mince

1 teaspoon ground cinnamon

salt and freshly ground black pepper

chopped roast almonds or walnuts, to garnish (optional)

1 To make the houmous, crush the garlic with the dried chilli and a little salt until you have a smooth paste. Put the rinsed chickpeas in a food processor with the garlic paste and olive oil, and process until almost smooth. Using a spatula, push all the mixture down from the sides before adding the cayenne pepper, parsley, and lemon juice. Season with salt and pepper, and add the yogurt. With the motor running, gradually add the sunflower oil in a thin, steady stream until you have a smooth light paste. (If you want a slightly thinner consistency, simply add a little water.)

2 Heat a frying pan over a medium-high heat, add a little oil, and fry the lamb mince until brown and crispy. Sprinkle over the cinnamon and season well with salt and pepper. Stir through well.

3 Spoon the fried lamb into a well in the centre of the chickpea purée, and sprinkle with the extra chopped parsley. This is a delicious sauce that complements grilled meat, fish, or vegetables. Garnish with some chopped roasted almonds or walnuts (if using).

Shawi ras el hanut ghanmi
Spicy lamb chops

Serves 4–6

60g (2oz) butter	2 garlic cloves, crushed
½ teaspoon ground coriander	30 fresh coriander leaves, chopped
½ teaspoon ground nutmeg	30 fresh mint leaves, chopped
1 teaspoon ground ginger	juice of 1 lemon
½ teaspoon ground cardamom	12 trimmed lamb loin chops
large pinch of ground cloves	salt and freshly ground black pepper
½ teaspoon ground Lebanese spice mix (see p218)	

1 Gently melt the butter in a small saucepan over a medium heat. Add the spices and fry for 2–3 minutes until aromatic. Add the garlic, fresh coriander, and mint. Mix together, then season well with salt and pepper. Add the lemon juice and remove from the heat. Leave to infuse in a warm place for at least 1 hour before using.

2 Heat a barbecue, griddle pan, or overhead grill until very hot. Season the lamb with salt and pepper, then brush with the infused spice mixture. When the barbecue or grill has reached a high heat, grill the lamb for 4–5 minutes on each side, continuing to baste frequently with the spicy butter to keep the meat moist and impart lots of flavour. (Infusing the spices in a warm place so that all the flavours combine and basting frequently are the keys to making this dish a rousing success.) Grill until the meat is crispy and brown on the outside, but still pink on the inside. Enjoy straight away.

This spice mixture bears similarities to a tandoor recipe from India and demonstrates the way in which ingredients follow much the same migration patterns as people, as well as displaying the influences that have passed from one part of the Muslim world to another. If you grind the spices yourself from whole, you achieve a much more aromatic result. Buy an electric coffee grinder just for spices. You can then grind your spices to order and make your own blends. You could use this recipe for lamb steaks, chicken drumsticks or skewers, or pork or beef to great effect.

Luz biskwi
Almond and cardamom biscuits

Makes 20–30 biscuits

300g (10oz) flour

45g (1½oz) butter, cut into chunks

1 tablespoon orange flower water

100g (3½oz) almonds, fried until golden,
  then ground

3 green cardamom pods

sugar to taste

vegetable oil for frying

These simple-to-make little biscuits work very well with a strong cup of coffee or some fresh mint tea. The flavour combination of cardamom, orange flower water, and roasted nuts is very emotive of the Middle East and conjures up images of spice markets, silks, and artefacts.
The biscuits are delicious with a cream- or milk-based pudding such as panna cotta or Turkish rice pudding. You could use a different sort of nut such as pistachios or hazelnuts, and cinnamon or nutmeg can be substituted for the cardamom.

1 Sift the flour into a large bowl, and rub the butter into the flour with your fingertips until the mixture is the texture of breadcrumbs. Add the orange flower water and a little cold water, just enough to make a smooth, soft dough. Cut the dough into small pieces, and open them out with finger and thumb so that you have uneven semi-flattened shapes. Fry in small batches for a few minutes until golden brown. Drain on kitchen paper.

2 Using a pestle and mortar, first grind the roasted almonds, then the cardamom pods. Mix the almonds, cardamom, and sugar together, and shake the fried dough pieces in the mixture until coated. Serve warm or cold, as a snack or with coffee or tea, or alongside a milk or cream dessert such as good-quality ice cream or a set custard.

The Menus

The Menus

Despite the enormous variety and diversity of street food from many countries, there are some common threads that run throughout. One of them is the communal nature of how the food is eaten. The food, the condiments, and the whole experience are shared by groups of friends and family – from eating some *mezze* in the Middle East to enjoying *chaat* in South India. People meet after work and before they head home, sharing contrasting dishes to create an intimate occasion. Alternatively, large groups can often be found eating en masse from the same stall.

I found one such example of this phenomenon in Salvador de Bahia in the northeast of Brazil. A dish with virtual cult status in this baroque city is *acaraje*. These delicious spicy bean patties are eaten late in the evening by hundreds of people at various stalls, before they all head out to party the night away in true Brazilian fashion. One particular stall that I visited was situated on the corner of a large square. There was seating for about 400 people in all, and the place was packed. The *acaraje* and their traditional accompaniments of salty dried prawns and hot and sour salad came from just that single stall. The surrounding cafés and bars were providing the beers, coconut juice, and other drinks, and at midnight the place was pumping. I had similar "mass-market" experiences of street food many times during my research for the book. What these experiences of delicious food from all over the world showed me was the importance of sharing food with friends. The shared experience of street food, of passing plates and eating together, encourages personal connections, and I wanted to create a menu section to show how this could be done for different occasions. There are so many types and styles of street food that can be eaten at any time of the day or night. They will work for picnics, barbecues, or those occasions when you are serving food without plates, such as canapé and finger-food parties. Street food can be used for light lunches or cosy nights in, or more formal dinner parties. Depending on the complexity of the event, there are dishes that can happily be used for each.

In this section, I have put together groups from the same region and also from further afield, but which use similar principles of cooking or may have some complementary or contrasting flavours. These menus are a simple guide, to show how a number of dishes can be combined to entice and satisfy your guests. I encourage you to be creative and experiment with your own choices for special meals to be shared by friends or family. Dipping into the bounty of delicious choices from different cuisines, and putting them in the context of entertaining at home, brings its own rewards and will satisfy both the appetite and the imagination.

Picnic

Street food is great for a picnic because it is very easy to transport, and the hamper will be much lighter on the return journey because everything will have been eaten with no waste. Whether you are meeting in the park, on the beach, on a hilltop, or at the races, the delectable contents of your hamper will prove the envy of all around because of its culinary diversity. A picnic made up of street food specialities will be far more memorable than some sandy cheese sandwiches or plain cold chicken. Instead, conjure up images of Mediterranean holidays, ancient spice routes, and oriental feasts. Pack your food, don't forget your refreshing drinks and fresh crusty bread, and most of all enjoy your day.

Menu 1

Potato, sausage, and semi-dried tomato pizza Italy pp136–7

Carrot and orange salad Morocco pp170–1

Libyan pumpkin dip Libya pp182–3

Houmous with cinnamon lamb Lebanon pp188–9

Harissa mini fish cakes with preserved lemon Morocco pp150–1

Menu 2

Grilled spring onions wrapped in pancetta Italy pp116–17

Flat bread, pumpkin paste, carrot pickle Afghanistan pp152–5

Poussin stuffed with olives, onion, and rosemary Italy pp120–1

Courgette salad Morocco p158

Date pastries Malta pp138–9

The style of food used for a picnic is very pick-up-able, and you will not need an excess of plates, knives, or forks. spread out the contents of your hamper and enjoy impressing your friends with the bright colours, contrasting textures, and delicious flavours of your repast.

Menu 3

Savoury ricotta-filled pastries Malta pp118–19

Lamb kebabs with tomato and white bean salad Turkey pp176–7

Green tomato salsa with chorizo in a tortilla wrap Mexico pp104–5

Toasted pitta bread salad Lebanon pp156–7

Sweet fried ravioli Italy pp122–3

Menu 4

Spinach pastries Lebanon pp164–5

Grilled tuna, sprouting broccoli, and ricotta calzone Italy p135

Barbecue jerk chicken with pineapple salsa Jamaica pp92–3

Spiced tomato relish Turkey p184

Spiced roast almonds Syria pp180–1

Top right: Potato, sausage, and semi-dried tomato pizza;
bottom left: Carrot and orange salad

Barbecue

From Turkey to Singapore, Ecuador to Vietnam, many street food dishes are grilled on outside barbecues and grills. The methods of grilling vary as much as the ingredients, marinades, spice rubs, and recipes. Street food lends itself very well to the home or portable barbecue, and it is perfect for summer evenings or lazy weekends. Aromatic plumes of smoke often guided me to stalls selling delicious items that epitomized the countries that I visited. I smelt where I was going long before I saw the meat, fish, cheese, or vegetable ready to be devoured with the aid of nothing more than a pile of crumpled paper napkins. Anticipation of the food to be eaten creates a great sense of atmosphere. Your guests will be salivating.

Menu 1

Grilled salty cheese marinated with oregano Brazil pp88–9

Spicy lamb chops Morocco pp190–1

Grilled artichokes with garlic, chilli, and pine nuts Italy pp128–9

Fresh peach salsa Mexico pp94–5

Green cashew nut sauce Brazil p107

The beauty of a barbecue is that, even though the preparation, marinating, and lighting of the thing may take some time, the actual cooking of the food is quick, and the results are instantly gratifying.

Menu 2

Summer rolls Vietnam pp44–5

Mango, papaya, and pineapple salad Singapore pp58–9

Chinese barbecue pork China pp 66–7

Skewers of beef with green chilli sauce Thailand pp62–3

Hot and sour squid and green mango salad Vietnam pp68–9

Menu 3

Chaat with green chilli and pomegranate India pp36–7

Seared steak with chimichurri Argentina p97

Spiced grilled chicken with coconut cream Malaysia pp76–7

Courgette salad Morocco p158

Sweet potato and pumpkin doughnuts Ecuador pp98–9

Menu 4

Grilled spring onions wrapped in pancetta Italy pp116–17

Lamb kebabs with white bean and tomato salad Turkey pp176–7

Grilled sardines Turkey pp144–5

Sesame salad Syria p159

Green tomato salsa Mexico pp104–5

Top right: Fresh peach salsa; bottom left: Grilled salty cheese marinated with oregano; bottom right: Spicy lamb chops

Leisurely lunch

The sharing of street food really brings the community together. In countries in the Middle East and Southeast Asia, you will often see family and friends all enjoying street food dishes as a group. The party may span several generations, from revered greatgrandparents to the youngest additions to the family clan. Sharing different dishes of street food makes for a very informal, relaxed type of meal; it is the food that brings everyone together. There is something for everyone to dip into while catching up on each other's lives. Different textures and flavours build a colourful mixture of contrasts – much like the family or friends who are enjoying the meal.

Menu 1

Chard soup with rice and turmeric Jordan pp148–9
Hot and sour grilled beef salad Vietnam pp72–3
Lamb meatballs with sour cherry sauce Turkey pp162–3
Smoky roast aubergine dip Lebanon p168
Sweet fried ravioli Italy pp122–3

Menu 2

Chicken-stuffed flat bread with curry sauce Singapore pp46–48
Eastern jewelled pilaf Jordan pp160–1
Salad of roast pork with cucumber Vietnam pp78–9
Houmous with cinnamon lamb Lebanon pp188–9
Toasted pitta bread salad Lebanon p154–155

Some of the best food in the world is the simplest and eaten by the people who have the least. Peasant and street food cooks from all over the world have to be much more resourceful to create delicious food because they do not have luxury ingredients at their disposal. You can apply similar principles to an informal lunch, where the food should be simple yet packed full of flavour.

Menu 3

Salt cod croquettes Spain p130–1
Coriander marinated fish Morocco pp174–5
Potato and cumin curry India pp38–9
Spinach and walnut salad Syria pp176–7
Almond and cardamom biscuits Morocco pp192–3

Menu 4

Spicy mussel soup Brazil pp86–7
Crispy paratha India pp34–5
Spicy fried okra Sri Lanka pp32–3
Courgettes stuffed with lamb and pine nuts Syria pp186–7
Yogurt cream cheese dip Lebanon p169

Top left: Hot and sour grilled beef salad; bottom left: Smoky roast aubergine dip; bottom right: Lamb meatballs with sour cherry sauce

Cosy night in

Street food is often thought of simply as snacks eaten in the fingers, but there are also much more elaborate dishes that constitute a whole meal. When transported into your home, they provide something completely different than the fare found at your average dinner party. If you like, serve the dishes in a continuous stream, as they are ready. This is similar to the Asian style of eating where there is really no break and definition between courses. It is a very relaxed way of dining, as each guest has a bowl or small plate, and chooses whatever he or she wants to eat. The meal is not rushed, with breaks between dishes while another dish is prepared, leaving time for chatting. Your guests will definitely be impressed.

Menu 1

Spicy bean soup Morocco pp166–7

Marinated quail with caper sauce Italy pp132–3

Eastern jewelled pilaf Jordan pp160–1

Spinach and walnut salad Syria pp176–7

Pumpkin pudding Brazil pp108–9

Menu 2

Mexican pumpkin flower soup Mexico pp100–1

Pan-fried red mullet Italy pp124–5

Stuffed aubergine with yogurt and pine nuts Lebanon p146

Carrot and orange salad Morocco pp170–1

Date pastries Malta pp138–9

For a different approach, take your guests on an undulating journey of contrasting tastes in the form of small courses that do not leave you too full at the end of the meal. You could match each course with a different wine to make a really special event.

Menu 3

Coconut and turmeric fish soup Sri Lanka pp26–7

Potato and cumin curry India pp38–9

Paper-wrapped chicken Malaysia pp52–3

Fresh coriander and peanut chutney Sri Lanka p31

Sichuan-style vegetable stir-fry China pp54–5

Menu 4

Spicy seasoned potato in a cone India pp28–30

Stuffed fish balls Lebanon p147

Grilled artichokes with garlic, chilli, and pine nuts Italy pp128–9

Bean patties with avocado and tomato salad Brazil pp90–1

Honey and nut pastries Italy pp126–7

Top left: Spicy bean soup; top right: marinated quail with caper sauce; bottom right: Pumpkin pudding

Drinks party

Street food can work very well in the form of
finger food or canapés for drinks parties. The
key to this sort of food is to ensure the right
balance of the four main flavours of hot, sweet,
salty, and sour in one mouthful. Several food
styles can be represented without confusion,
and the food can emerge from the kitchen
throughout the evening, as hot and fresh as
from the best street food stalls. What also
works brilliantly is having a combination
of different sorts of foods that are all fully
flavoured, but of varying complexity. Dips
and pastes, for example, are delicious but very
simple to put together. Instead of going for
more elaborate dishes, serve the more rustic
choices that will still knock your guests for six.

Menu 1

Masala popadums with tomato and green chilli India pp24–5

Indonesian beef sate skewers Indonesia p49

Lebanese lamb pizza Lebanon pp172–3

Harissa mini fish cakes with preserved lemon Morocco pp150–1

Savoury ricotta-filled pastries Malta pp118–19

When it comes to displaying finger food for your guests' eating pleasure, arrange individual items in odd numbers. If there are three or five of any one thing on a serving plate or platter, your eyes and fingers are drawn to them because they look interesting and imperfect. If the numbers are even, people hesitate to spoil the symmetry.

Menu 2

Spicy seasoned potato in a cone India pp28–30

Seafood empanadas Ecuador pp102–3

Crispy chicken spring rolls Vietnam pp60–1

Semolina flour fritters Italy pp114–15

Libyan pumpkin dip Libya pp182–3

Menu 3

Paper-wrapped chicken Malaysia pp52–3

Prawn fritters with sweet chilli sauce Singapore pp56–7

Potato, sausage, and semi-dried tomato pizza Italy pp136–7

Spiced tomato relish Turkey p184

Spinach pastries Lebanon pp164–5

Menu 4

Summer rolls Vietnam pp46–7

Chaat with green chilli and pomegranate India pp36–7

Skewers of beef with green chilli sauce Thailand pp62–3

Salt cod croquettes Spain pp130–1

Spiced roast almonds Syria pp180–1

Top left: Indonesian beef sate skewers;
bottom right: Masala popadums with tomato and green chilli

Glossary

bok choy Part of the Brassica family, bok choy is also known as Chinese white cabbage and white mustard cabbage. It is used in salads and stir-fries.

Chinese cabbage Also called napa cabbage, celery cabbage, and Peking cabbage, Chinese cabbage is part of the mustard family. Not to be confused with bok choy, it is used in salads and stir-fries.

chipotle Chipotle chillies are dried and smoked ripe jalapeño chillies. Commonly used throughout Mexico, chipotles are available in several forms: as a powder, as whole dried chipotle pods, in a can as *chipotle en adobo* (combined with other spices as a paste), or as a concentrated paste. Chipotle is available from Latin American grocers or gourmet food stores.

choy sum Another member of the cabbage family, choy sum is also called flowering white cabbage and Chinese flowering cabbage. It is used in salads and stir-fries, and is available from Asian and Chinese grocers, and better greengrocers.

fish sauce This pungent liquid made from fermented anchovies or other fish is an essential Southeast Asian ingredient. It loses its fishiness on cooking, mellowing to add flavour. Recipes vary, but can be used interchangeably. Known as nam pla in Thailand and nuoc nam in Vietnam, it is available from good supermarkets and Asian grocers.

galangal Especially popular in Thai cuisine, galangal is a hot and peppery aromatic rhizome. A little like ginger root, it is used as a seasoning throughout Southeast Asia. It is available in both root and dried form from Asian grocers.

harissa This fiery paste made from chillies, garlic, and spices is found in supermarkets and Middle Eastern grocers. It can be bought in a tube which looks like tomato purée, or in cans or jars; you can also buy it as a dry spice mix and make your own by adding tomato purée (paste), lemon, and salt.

masa harina This flour is ground from corn kernels that have first been soaked in limewater, then dried. This is the process that makes it differ from ordinary cornmeal. *Masa* is traditionally used to make corn tortillas. *Masa harina* is used in Central and South American cooking, and is available from Latin American grocers.

Lebanese spice mix This term can be quite ambiguous, as each chef has his or her personal recipe. A guideline is 4 parts ground cinnamon, 1 part ground cloves, 1 part chilli powder, and 1 part ground cardamom. Grind your own using a coffee grinder, store in an airtight jar, and use as needed.

mooli Also known as daikon, Japanese radish, Chinese radish, or Oriental radish, this long root vegetable has crisp white flesh; the skin is either creamy white or black. Look for mooli with unwrinkled skin. Mooli can be used raw in salads or as a garnish, or cooked in stir-fries. It is available from Indian, Asian, and Japanese grocers.

palm oil Extracted from the fruit of the African palm, this reddish-orange oil is very high in saturated fats. Commonly used in Brazilian cooking, especially in Bahia, it has a distinctive flavour and should not be mistaken for the milder and lighter palm kernel oil.

palm sugar This sugar is made from the sap of date or coconut palms. It is also known as coconut sugar, gur, and jaggery. In India, the term *jaggery* also refers to sugar refined from raw sugarcane.

pimentón Pimentón is a smoked paprika and comes in two varieties: *pimentón dulce* (sweet and mild) and *pimentón picante* (hot). It is available from good supermarkets and Latin American grocers.

pomegranate molasses A fantastic Middle Eastern ingredient, pomegranate molasses comes in bottles. A thick, dark syrup made from the reduced juice of puréed pomegranates, it is fabulously sour and sweet at the same time, similar to a very good quality aged balsamic vinegar. If not available, substitute a little reduced good-quality balsamic vinegar.

queijo de coalho A Brazilian cheese, *queijo de coalho* is similar in taste and texture to haloumi, which works well as an alternative.

sambal oelek A *sambal* is a spicy and fiery paste made primarily from chillies, which is served as a condiment. Used in Southeast Asian cooking, particularly in Indonesia, Singapore, and Malaysia, there are several forms. One is *sambal oelek* (perhaps the most basic), which is made with chillies, brown sugar, and salt. It is available in jars from Asian grocers.

shrimp paste Made from salted fermented prawns, shrimp paste comes in a block and has a strong taste and pungent smell, which dissipates on cooking to become aromatic. Recipes vary slightly depending on where it is made. It should be used only sparingly and is available from Asian grocers.

sour cherry The sour cherry (*Prunus cerasus*) is smaller than its sweet counterpart, and comes in several varieties, including Aleppo, Montmorency, and Morello. Fresh sour cherries are usually available from late spring to early summer. Fresh sour cherries from the Aleppo region can be difficult to come by unless you have a good Middle Eastern grocer nearby. Dried sour cherries are a perfect substitute and are found in good supermarkets.

sumac A dark red berry, sumac is dried and ground into a coarse powder that is almost purple in colour and has a very distinctive peppery, sour, and slightly bitter flavour. Commonly used in cooking of the Levant and Middle East, it is treated as a condiment like pepper. It is available from Middle Eastern grocers and health-food stores. If you cannot find it, use lots of black pepper and lemon juice in its place.

tamarind This is an essential ingredient in Indian and Southeast Asian cooking, and is also found in Middle Eastern and Persian recipes. The fruit of the tamarind are large pods yielding both seeds and a tart pulp. Used as a flavouring in much the same way as lemon juice, the pulp comes in concentrated form in jars, as a paste, in a dried brick, or as a powder. It is available from Indian, Asian, and some Middle Eastern grocers.

Thai basil This has a different flavour to ordinary basil and is quite like aniseed. If not available, substitute a combination of fresh coriander and mint leaves.

Useful Websites

India and Sri Lanka

www.deepakfoods.com

www.indianspiceshop.com

www.simplyspice.co.uk

www.tamleni.com

www.hindustan.com.au

China and Southeast Asia

www.cuisinenet.co.uk/tajstores/

www.thaladthai.co.uk

www.wingyip.com

www.asianfoods.com.au

www.tqc-burlington.com.au

Latin America and the Caribbean

www.mexgrocer.co.uk

www.scorchio.co.uk

www.coolchile.co.uk

www.caribbean-food.co.uk

Middle East and North Africa

www.belazu.com

www.seasonedpioneers.co.uk

General

www.hardtofindfoods.co.uk

www.thespiceshop.co.uk

Index

Acknowledgments

Author

Thank you to Mary-Clare Jerram, Carl Raymond, and Monika Schlitzer for seeing the potential in my writing. To Borra Garson and Martine Carter at Deborah McKenna Ltd. Thank you to Dawn Henderson, Siobhán O'Connor, Susan Downing, Simon Daley, and Julia Kepinska, and the fantastic teams at DK. Thank you to Lisa Linder for her spectacular photographs and Alice Hart for making such delicious food, and to Jasmine Hart for growing (and delivering) the pumpkin flowers.

Huge appreciation to the people around the world who so generously helped in my pursuit of this book. First to Heather Paterson, who makes my life work, and Toni Vallenduuk of Flight Centre. In Ecuador, Alegría Plaza, Maria Clara Perez and her family, Marita Uribe, and Fernando Perez; from Argentina, Alicia and Jose Que Sada, Hugh and Celina Arnold; the Brazilians for showing me such a good time, Silvania Presta, Bec and Michel Saad, Gabi Kropacsy and her mum for showing me the real samba in Rio. Stuart Campbell and Bina Shah for their contacts. Sara Grasso for showing me culinary Sicily. In Malta, big thanks to Michael Zammit Tobana, owner of the Fortina Spa Resort, and to the chefs at Taste, at the Fortina, who cook my food so well. A massive thank you to Ratnesh and his family, and to Jaimin and Amandip Kotecha.

In Morocco, thanks to Richard and Sophie and Oliver Neat at the magnificent Casa Lalla in Marrakesh. In Lebanon, huge thanks to May and Nasser Nakib, and Talal Daouk for generously hosting us. A round of applause to Suha and to Kifah Arif for introductions to her family across the Middle East. Ronnie and Serj Hochar from Chateau Musar for their love of the flavours of life. In Jordan, Ali Najaf and family for a trip of wonders. In Turkey, Elizabeth Hewitt for being my eating companion, and Muhammet and Omer Solak for the incredible generosity of their family.

To the great cooks who have inspired me – Rose Gray and Ruth Rogers at the River Café, Rick Stein, Loyd Grossman, Peter Doyle from Est in Sydney, and David

Thompson. To Tim Lee and Ashley Huntington for keeping the food debate wide open, Danielle and Rafael Fox Brinner, Bernie Plaisted (for being my best man in the kitchen), JJ Holland, Charlie Mash, Sarah Rowden, Clare Kelly, Birgit Erath and Celia Brooks Brown. To Chantal Rutherford Brown, the Cutting Edge School of Food and Wine, Books for Cooks, Susan Pieterse, Tertia Goodwin, all at Leiths, Liz Trigg, Toby Peters, Peter Durose, Helen Chislet. To Matt Maddocks, Wye Yap, Peter Harman, and everyone in Sydney. To Debbie Wallen, Annette Peters, and Helena Flemming at Marks & Spencer. To all the chefs and friends who make it so much fun. This is for you.

Picture Credits

The publisher would like to thank the following for their kind permission to reproduce their photographs:

(a-above; b-below; c-centre; f-far; l-left; r-right; t-top)

Alamy Images: Nick Baylis 40; Pat Behnke 140; Mike Booth 154; CuboImages srl 113bl, 113br; Danita Delimont 72; eStock Photo 62; Food Alan King 23br; Peter Forsberg 24; Doug Houghton 57; La Belle Aurore 31; Manor Photography 38; Adrian Muttitt 20, 36; PCL 23tl; Picture Contact 120; Robert Harding Picture Library Ltd 110; Alex Segre 35; Jochen Tack 76; Tribaleye Images / J Marshall 82; **Corbis:** zefa / Peter Adams 23tr; **Getty Images:** Gallo Images / Heinrich van den Berg 29; The Image Bank / Stuart Westmorland 23bl; Purestock 26; Robert Harding World Imagery / Amanda Hall 32; **PunchStock:** Brand X Pictures 169

All other travel images © Tom Kime

Jacket images: Front: Getty Images: The Image Bank / John Lund tr; Lonely Planet Images / Paul Beinssen ftr; National Geographic / Richard Nowitz ftl; Stone / Simon Watson tl

All other images © Dorling Kindersley

Thanks also to Magimix for equipment supplied for the photographic shoot.

For further information see: www.dkimages.com